Melody in Living Together

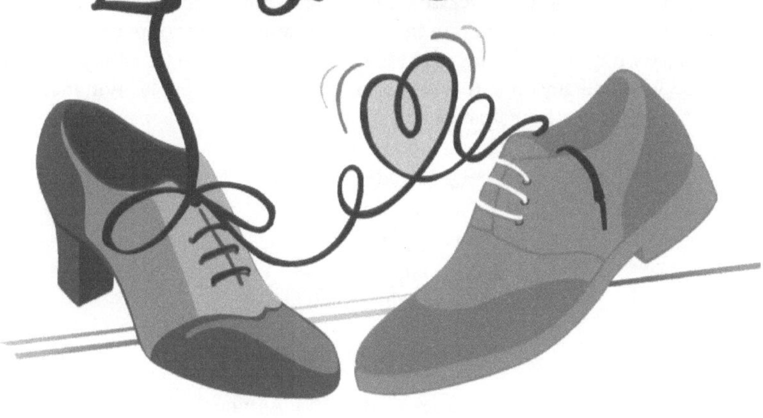

Dr. Pratibha Deshpande

Writing assistance: Dr. Arti Kurra,
Dr. Vvishakha Barve

MELODY IN LIVING TOGETHER

Sakal Media Pvt. Ltd.
595, Budhwar Peth,
Pune – 411002, India

www.sakalpublications.com
sakalprakashan@esakal.com

First Edition: 24 May 2024

ISBN No.: 978-81-973384-5-8

Edited by: Manjula Shukla

Cover Design & Typesetting: Madhumita Shinde

Printed in India by Sakal Media Pvt. Ltd.

It is the eve of our golden jubilee together.

I want to give you a gift,

That will never fade and will last forever.

To honour our everlasting love and commitment,

The many happy moments I have treasured with you.

We found our melody.

Dilip, my dear

This is a book for you here.

From a Counsellor's Pen to the Reader's Eye

Counselling involves transformation. It is a process of discovery and growth of understanding and healing.

My firm opinion is that self-discovery is the key to leading a happy life. Identifying areas for improvement and setting future goals can be achieved through regular self-reflection. Also, it helps one gain a deeper understanding of one's strengths and weaknesses.

My thoughts are reflected in my two books: "Before You Find a Counsellor" and "Swayam 365". This is the third book in the series.

Whenever someone asks me how society is formed, I reply that it is formed by people, their collective beliefs, values, cultures, economic systems, and political structures. Cultural practices, traditions, and individual growth are all part of it. Family structure affects a society's climate, happiness, and well-being.

My thoughts about society and family spirit encouraged me to write this book. The harmony of a family depends on the dynamism of the couple. The relationship between life partners is beautiful if nurtured and maintained for a lifetime.

There are many benefits if these relationships are long-term and harmonious. The next generation will inherit a happy family structure. It will be a conducive environment for them to grow up in. Their nurturing is done in a stable and secure environment.

Parents can create a sense of belonging by being positive role models, supporting and guiding them. They will establish boundaries and rules for them. Ultimately, they will be able to grow and develop into strong individuals. Planting seeds and caring for the saplings will ensure that family trees are healthy, bear sweet fruits, and provide shade for future generations.

Having this feeling in my heart as a counsellor, I was inspired to write a book to spread this message.

Friends, this is the story behind the book.

It wasn't my cup of tea to undertake this mission alone. This journey was made possible by many of my seekers, relatives and friends.

Strong pillars were Dr Arti and Dr Vvishakha for assisting me in writing. The support I received from Dr Shuchita and Dr Sanjivani was greatly appreciated. Nivedita Gonge, Achala Sabne, Ashwini Nandeshwar, Rucha Dhayrikar, Rohini Barve were always with me, giving valuable feedback.

My editors, Manjula Shukla and Ashwini Mahajan, transformed this script into one that is clearer and more concise.

A scientific and artistic approach to the book was transformed into a creative art piece by Madhumita Shinde. By capturing the book's emotions and insights, she transformed them into a captivating work of art. Thank you Madhumita.

Most importantly, I have no idea how to thank my publisher, Sakal Media. Since day one, they have been my unwavering supporters, and I appreciate their belief in me and my work. They have gone out of their way to make me successful, and I cannot thank them enough. This book is the 7th in a row, and every experience confirms my opinion. I would like to thank Sakal Media and their staff for encouraging me, supporting and believing in me. Each of the books was praised by readers as well as critics.

One of the reasons I am so confident about my statement about Sakal Media is the fact that my book 'Swayam 365' won the publishers' first prize in the category of useful and novel book.

The book was praised for its innovative approach to teaching self-worth and comprehensive understanding of the subject. It has been a runaway success.

Sakal Media, thank you for being my backbone.

No project is enjoyable without my family and friends. My special thanks go out to my seekers. We have a two-way relationship. Both of us teach each other.

In what capacity am I entitled to write this book?

First, I am a counsellor. Secondly, my husband and I have enjoyed growing old together for 50 years. As fine wine, our relationship has matured and become more flavourful with age.

In our life together, I gained insights into the secrets of harmonious relationships.

Each line has its own message.

The art and science of healthy relationships go hand in hand. Adapt the ideas which are based on psychology and live together happily.

Regards,

- Dr Pratibha Deshpande
9890169559
dilippratibha@gmail.com

My story

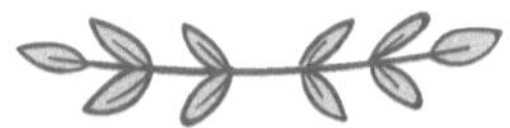

Today was the golden anniversary of their marriage, yes!
On the beautifully decorated table, a covered cake was placed. The discussion was on how the cake should be. He said to ask her and she said to ask him.

When asked both they replied,
'We need a cake substantial enough to serve all the couples who think they can't get along because they are not compatible.'
On the top of cake was written,
'Melody in living together.'

She said,
"We could create a beautiful world because we are different,
Because we are different, our world has many colours.
Colour has different shades because we are different.
There are golden and silver fringes on those shades."
He said, "I am silver, and she is gold."
"This isn't the case," she said.
"Since he accepted silver, I became golden.
'Our universe is complete' because our relationships are melodious."

How was she when they met?

A twenty-year-old bubbly girl, from rich parents, a one-child family, always surrounded by friends, an extrovert, open to new experiences, not thinking of marriage because she was studious, intelligent, with big dreams, and enjoying her own world. She was a Metro girl who expressed her opinions boldly and talked fearlessly. Traveling and exploring new places was her passion, as well as music and literature. As an independent well-versed girl, she always wanted to do things her way. She was inspiring and enthusiastic.

And he?

An engineer, coming from a simple middle-class family with educational values, shy, not speaking much, and introverted. He was the youngest of nine siblings. Incapable of expressing his opinions, his dreams were small. He never felt appreciated because his family had no time for him. He was satisfied with his life and what his family expected of him. Despite the obstacles he faced, he was determined to succeed.

A romantic relationship was unknown to her.

He was looking for a bride who was undemanding, he wanted to live a simple life. He wanted someone who understood him and accepted him as he was.

There was no sign of compatibility between them. Therefore, they ignored being compatible and acknowledged their similarities, and what magic happened, they became compatible.

Today they are celebrating their fifty glorious years of togetherness.

Contents

Section 1

Being Together

1. Being Together

2. From First Glance till Forever

1

Being Together

Where romantic movies end, this book begins. It is a fairytale that they lived happily ever after. However, life is not always a fantasy. There are lots of twists and turns, sometimes it is a bed of roses, sometimes we need to walk on thorns. All the answers are in this book. Couples can use it to navigate their relationship, weather any storm and come out stronger. There is a roadmap to a successful and fulfilling living together.

'The Magnificence of Love,' written by Rumi, is a timeless poem of love and devotion.

Rumi says… "Your magnificence has made me wonder. Your charm has taught me the way of love."

When we hear love songs, we get goosebumps. We miss and crave the company of our loved ones. There is something special about this relationship. It takes many forms and has different shades and colours.

No matter what the relationship is, legally married, live-in-relationship, or in romantic relationships, there is a different kind of fun in this relationship. This relationship, rooted in various forms, has vibrant flavours.

There are rich, greedy, faithful, and loving relationships, as well as faithful, deep, funny relationships or painful, conflicted relationships. Interestingly, we experience all these shades with the same partner at different times.

From first glance to forever love, how did the relationship begin?

There is an affinity for this relationship among all living things that has evolved through the ages. The relationship has taken many turns, but men and women have always been attracted to each other. First, a one-to-many partner, then a live-in relationship, (monogamous relationship) because live-in relationship had some shortcomings, finally marriage.

The marriage system formed by our ancestors was not fully reliable. There was a different time and a different set of needs back then. During that time, they developed the system based on what was essential and obvious. While they certainly had the progress of society in mind, in this scenario, women were neglected, perhaps unintentionally at first, but more intentionally later. It is not necessary to point out the mistakes or faults in the traditions when reviewing. Women were not given the same rights as men due to gender bias. Men were allowed more freedom to pursue careers, while women were expected to stay at home and take care of the family. Laws and customs of the time reflected this gender bias, as women were not allowed to own property or make financial decisions for themselves.

As a symbol of bravery, man provided for the needs like food, shelter, clothing, and safety for his family. The woman was to manage the household and raise the children. It was a division of labour based on natural abilities and tendencies of men and

women. With a view to create a stronger family dynamic and a more prosperous community, women were expected to take care of the house and children, while men were expected to provide for the family.

The husband was expected to think about his wife's happiness in this system. When women are respected and treated well, they are more likely to feel empowered and confident in their roles, allowing them to make positive and productive contributions to the community. The ripple effect occurs when the impact of one action spreads out further and further, ultimately leading to positive changes in all aspects of life for every member of the family.

The system has been in place for many years but has not produced the expected results. While it was based on natural tendencies, there were times when women were not respected and cared for, which had negative consequences. Due to an imbalance of power and respect, women felt devalued and treated as second class citizens, with fewer rights and opportunities than men.

Women faced mental health issues, abuse, and violence because they felt isolated, powerless, and undervalued. Often, these feelings were caused by gender inequality and limited access to resources and opportunities. In the absence of control and support, women felt helpless and overwhelmed, leading to a variety of mental health problems. Women were forced into marriage, often against their will. Marriage was used to secure and perpetuate men's power. It was possible for a man to gain control over a woman's property, labour, and children through marriage, all of which could be used to strengthen his own power. Because she was unable to support herself financially, she was reliant on others to provide her with food, clothing, and shelter. This was

especially true for women in patriarchal societies, where women were often denied the ability to own property or work. Though this statement sounds harsh, but it is true.

The marriage system was established to carry the progeny forward, where the man's name would continue. As a result, woman became a tool for propagation.

There were many revolutionaries who brought about changes in women's lives and their rights in the past. Over the past few years, there has been a lot of change seen. Women today are conquering every field because of their education. The change in gender roles has opened new career opportunities for women, allowing them to pursue careers they weren't previously able to pursue.

Women can stand on their own feet now. They do not have to suffer mental, physical, emotional torture at the hands of husbands or their in-laws anymore, they are aware of the injustice done so far and are claiming their proper place in society, expectations are rising. Women expect to hold the same position as men in society and in marriage and are striving for equal opportunities in the workplace, in education.

Women today are conveniently blamed for failure of marriage by saying they want freedom. This view ignores the fact that marriage is a two-way street, and that men must also come to understand and accept the new role of women in marriage.

Today's women have more freedom than ever before, and this freedom has enabled them to pursue careers and interests that were once off-limits. On the other hand, men have yet to adjust their expectations of what makes a good marriage. Marriages will continue to fail if men do not adjust, and women will be unfairly blamed.

It's time to change the male-dominated culture. Women and men should be treated equally and respectfully. Now marriage has two equal and competent players. Like earlier, a woman is no longer a secondary subject. This evolving situation must be taken into account when considering the institution of marriage. Only then will marriage have true meaning for living together, symbolizing a lifelong partnership between two people.

Views of the modern generation

We cannot deny the fact that the changing social tendencies influence the marriage system, but it has not lost its importance completely. Is the marriage system at risk? It may or may not be. Marriage is still a very important institution in many societies, and people still get married and have children. In terms of harmonizing and stabilizing society, it is the most reliable and trusted system so far.

But the tragedy is that the current generation views marriage as an invitation to tensions, punishments, liabilities, and many negative emotions entwined together as seen in the previous generation. Therefore, they doubt the importance of marriage.

Women have also started to consider whether they want to get married. It seems strange for her that she would want to spend her entire life serving her husband, in-laws, children, and grandchildren. Instead, she can live her life freely. And she asks herself if she really wants to continue the traditional marriage system that has suppressed her wishes, desires, progress, and hopes for so long. She feels insecure just thinking about marriage. Marriage is something she dreads. To get companionship in old age, is marriage essential? 'No' is the answer. Today, there are

many options for leading a solo life. It is becoming more and more common for women to give birth without getting entangled in relationships. Both men and women are adopting children as single parents.

Thus, many people have found solutions and are living their lives according to their requirements and ambitions. Instead of relying on what society expects from them, couples are focusing on building strong, meaningful relationships based on mutual respect, trust, and understanding. Nevertheless, the way it is conducted has changed significantly over time. There are many options available for men and women.

- Live-in-relationship, friendship, roommate.
- Solitary life.
- Fulfilling physical and emotional requirements as per need without getting tied in marriage.
- Exchanging gender-based roles, a father baby-sitting and mother earning; etc.

Take a moment to consider the irony of this change in the society. In the past, society moved from live-in-relationship to marriage to improve its quality of life. Now, we are again travelling back from marriage to live-in-relationship.

When we questioned the idea that both parents were necessary for a child's upbringing, once again, we returned to the olden days of single parenting. Single-parent households are becoming increasingly popular due to the changing social and economic landscape.

The concept of joint family was introduced to strengthen society, but now we look back and see joint family structure as a hindrance to progress. Historically, the joint family structure was

an important source of support and stability in society. Now that people have access to more resources, they can form a support outside of their families more easily. Consequently, many people now view joint family structure more negatively than positively and opt for a nuclear family.

Why are we going backwards?

Several factors explain this, but in a single sentence, it seems that "Marriage or joint family structure does not provide the benefits people expect."

What can be done to save marriage as an institution or is there anything more we can do to ensure that marriage remains a strong and valued institution for generations to come?

Although times have changed, the attraction between a man and a woman remains as primal as it ever was. Affinity, fondness, interest, etc., are also intertwined with it. Dimensions have only been widened. We shouldn't discard everything that is old, however. It will surely be more intense and meaningful if we are able to preserve some unique qualities from the marriage system and weave a relation around it.

Would it be possible to redefine the concept of marriage?

Certainly, if we consider romantic relationships based on new principles, new understanding for both partners and their relatives, we can redefine marriage again.

We can't forget the fact that this can be one of the most beautiful and meaningful relationships that will last a lifetime. A husband and wife's relationship are intricate yet affectionate, we can redefine marriage in a new way. What we need is to modify the rules of this game.

Since both players in this game are now highly educated, careerists, independent, and capable of living on their own. It is possible for them to come together and live a more beautiful life together if they decide to do so.

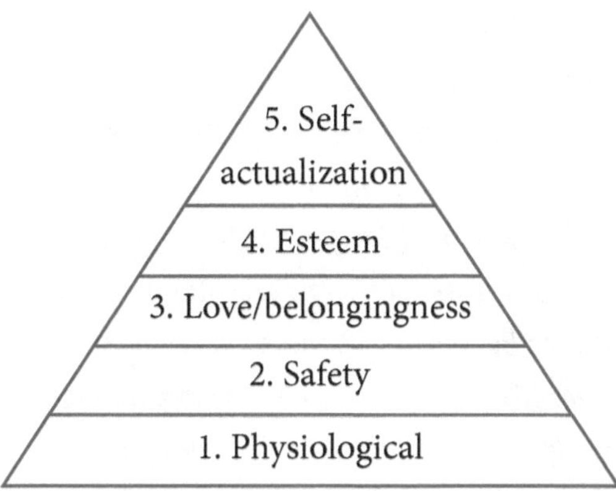

From the above figure, we can see that each of us has five basic needs, according to Maslow. When the woman was dependent on the man, marriage was essential to fulfill the initial two needs. In contrast, women today do not depend on their husbands to fulfill first two needs. She can easily fulfill this on her own.

Marriage is to emphasize equality, partnership, and mutual respect rather than traditional gender roles or religious norms. This could involve rethinking marital responsibilities, decision-making processes, and economic arrangements. Redefining marriage may involve incorporating diverse cultural and religious practices into legal frameworks while respecting individual rights and freedoms.

Marriage will benefit her only if her top three needs,

- Love, belongingness
- Self-esteem
- Self-actualization

especially, the need of 'self-actualization', are met. It's about realizing, understanding, and manifesting one's full potential.

Her marriage will survive only if her husband helps her, motivates her and supports her in fulfilling her top three needs.

For Example:

Fifty-three-year-old Rajni is stuck in her marriage of thirty years. Her husband, who is a lawyer and a very strict person by nature, doesn't care about her feelings and she must face his wrath whenever there is a situation that is not as per his desire because she is dependent on him for her needs. In contrast to this Rajni's daughter, Deepa, who is a twenty-six-year-old engineer and not dependent on anyone for her financial needs for food, shelter and clothing will not endure wrong behavior from her husband. This is the change we are talking about that has come to the girls of today.

It is more likely that women will have happy relationships if their partners support them, understand their needs, give them equal opportunity and provide emotional support.

2

From First Glance till Forever

Any relationship is a serious commitment that needs to take on a lot of responsibility and requires two people to support one another through thick and thin, lifelong. **A live-in relationship or a romantic relationship has fewer commitments than a marriage but for having a long-lasting relationship we need to be ready within.** We need to equip ourselves with the necessary knowledge, skills, and resources to handle the burden. It is important that we are mature enough to understand the scope of the obligations we are responsible for.

So, my dear, think before you take the big leap!

Are we able to take responsibility for relationships?

Here, we should consider 'the maturity age' before getting into a relationship, though the legal marriageable age is eighteen in most countries.

An individual's emotional, psychological, and spiritual maturity determines their maturity age. A mature individual is the one who make wise decisions, chooses his/her actions, understand the consequences of his/her actions, and is morally responsible. He/she is aware of values, beliefs and possesses good moral values.

He/she knows the true meaning of being in a relationship and respects his/her partner with pride.

The catch here is-someone may mature at eighteen, someone at forty and someone at eighty and, perhaps, someone never!

Before getting into a relationship, we need to make ourselves capable of taking responsibility since this relationship involves a lot of commitments.

Ancient and medieval Hindu scriptures have classified our life into four stages. These are:

- Brahmacharya (student)
- Vanaprastha (retirement)
- Grihastha (householder)
- Sannyasa (renunciation)

This framework is created by dividing our life into these four stages. At each stage, there are specific duties and tasks to be performed. They teach us the importance of dedication and hard work required at every stage. This book is about the second stage. To perform well in the second phase, it is necessary to pass the first one successfully.

The first stage is brahmacharya, Vidyarthi Dasha. In this we are expected to focus on our studies. We must control our worldly and sensual (physical pleasure and sex) desires by focusing on self-discipline. It teaches control over our senses and concentration on gaining wisdom. This stage emphasizes mental, physical and spiritual growth, working hard to gain knowledge.

If we progress well in this stage, the second stage is more likely to be happy and sweet.

From the perspective of a counsellor:

One thing that is important in the student stage is control of worldly and sensual desires.

Nowadays, this seems to be a rare occurrence. Counsellors find that men and women experience marital problems because of body pleasures at puberty or even earlier, and this definitely affects their future. It is not the only cause, but an important one.

Do I really want to get married?

It is important to decide what kind of relationship one wants before answering this question. A live-in relationship or a romantic relationship has fewer commitments than a marriage. If our answer is. "Yes, I want to get married," then the next question is, "Why Am I Getting Married?"

We can choose an answer from the following list or provide our own.

1. Marriage is customary and parents insist that we get married. Everyone gets married, so why do I delay or think about it?

2. Marriage is a wonderful way to be happy, it's important to continue the family name and have children, so marriage is important.

3. I need someone who is legally mine, with whom physical intimacy will be easy and free, where stability will be essential and sorrows will be shared.

4. The time has come for me to get married. I believe that marriage is a milestone in life and should be achieved between twenty-five and thirty years of age.

Marriage cannot be justified by all these reasons. Our marriage here is for convenience's sake and to gain something for personal happiness and pleasure. It is often believed that marriage is a way to achieve a certain level of financial stability, social acceptance, physical intimacy, and companionship. Some people

get married to gain status or access to certain resources, such as family connections or inheritances.

All these reasons are motivated by personal gain. Usually, one party hopes to gain some advantage. Marriage for convenience refers to relationships in which one party seeks to gain something from the relationship.

If that purpose is not served, then they are ready to dissolve the marriage. Marriage for love, however, is based on mutual respect and understanding. Neither party is motivated by material gain but by emotional attachment. The strength and longevity of love-based marriages can be attributed to this.

Is it right to get married without ever considering 'Why I want to get married?' and 'Do I really want to get married?' How can we be so casual about something like marriage?'It is a commitment that lasts a lifetime.

Before getting married, it is essential to determine our level of physical, emotional, mental, intellectual, social, and economic willingness. A marriage cannot be based solely on the continuation of family name and descendants.

Are we getting married only to have a companion, friend, and Partner. Yes, a very noble thought. But is this the case for everyone? In most marriages, the husband remains a husband for life, while the wife remains a wife forever. True?

Does that mean we shouldn't get married?

That's not the case at all! We need to decide if we want to marry for traditional reasons or do we have our own criteria?

For example:

Sunil's criteria was, "It is time for me to get married. I am educated and have a good job. At this time, I am ready to

take responsibility for my Partner's needs, which is why I want to get married. I value the secure financial position I have and would like a close and happy relationship with my future Partner. It is important to me that I have a trusted friend, a companion, and a Partner with whom I can share all of my emotions. I want to establish a meaningful and lasting relationship with someone who understands me and loves me unconditionally. It is important to me that I find someone who is loyal, kind, and values trust. I need someone who will be my rock and help me grow. I am aware that my Partner will also have the same or more expectations from me. I am mentally physically and emotionally prepared to meet those expectations. I will also value my Partner's goal, aspirations and desires. We will create a harmonious world together. Our goal will be to make a lasting positive impact on our family by working together. We will support each other in times of difficulty and celebrate our achievements. Through life's ups and downs, we will create a strong bond. I am sure that together we will create melody in our life."

Sunil is thinking in the right direction. He understands the meaning of marriage. He is ready to take responsibility, he is ready to fulfil his Partner's wishes.

However, he also has too many expectations from his Partner. It is possible that he expects his Partner to be perfect in every way. Does it make sense to have so many expectations of a Partner? Maybe he should focus on himself and make sure he meets his own expectations before expecting anything from his Partner. He might become frustrated if he doesn't find what he's looking for.

There is no such thing as a perfect Partner. Getting a tailor-made Partner is not possible. We can keep our expectations, but we cannot count on them being met. Everyone is unique and brings something different to the table.

Is it right to have so many expectations from our Partner?

It depends on how severe the expectations are. It is okay to have them if they are reasonable and attainable. In contrast, if they are too high and impossible to meet, it can lead to frustration and disappointment.

It's important to consider aspects such as compatibility, commitment, communication, shared values, and long-term goals. Some people find fulfilment and happiness in marriage, while others may prefer other forms of commitment or happily remain single.

Setting expectations is important for creating a mutual understanding between two Partners by creating a sense of trust and security, as well as ensuring that both Partners are on the same page. It is, however, important to make sure expectations are not too high, unreasonable, or impossible to meet.

Marriage does not mean doing everything together all the time. Each Partner needs a space to be alone and pursue their own interests. Keeping a healthy balance in a relationship is also important, as each person has their own needs. Being alone with oneself and with the other person, both are equally important.

A Partner who has too many expectations can put unnecessary pressure on the other Partner and ultimately pressure on the relationship, leading to disappointment and resentment. To maintain a successful relationship, it is important to set realistic expectations that may or may not be met. Finding

a balance between what each of you can realistically accomplish is important. It can also be harmful to set too few expectations from your Partner. If you don't expect anything from your Partner, you may not feel appreciated or needed. Feelings of loneliness and isolation can further damage your relationship. It is like setting boundaries in a healthy friendship. Boundaries allow both people to feel like they have their own space and freedom, while still being able to rely on one another for support when needed.

Long-term Relationships are Beneficial

For any romantic relationship, the principle is the same. Their lives are shared. Together, they support each other in their endeavours and cherish their special moments. Their relationship is characterized by physical intimacy, and many times it goes way beyond the physical act itself. A deep connection allows both partners to feel vulnerable, loved, and desired. They can express their emotions and strengthen their bond through it. A long-term relationship allows us to grow together and gives us security in life.

What are the benefits of having a long-term relationship?

It is important to have a long-lasting relationship because it provides stability and security for both parties. Also, it provides emotional support and companionship, which can help people feel more connected and fulfilled. Relationships can provide a sense of comfort and belonging, which can reduce stress levels and improve overall health.

Is it advisable to have multiple romantic partners?

As you manage multiple relationships, you may experience feelings of insecurity and jealousy as well as increased stress. Furthermore, it can be challenging to give each partner the attention and time they need, which can lead to feelings of dissatisfaction.

Our body is a sacred temple, and it has various energies flowing in and out of it. If we have multiple romantic partners, then we will corrupt the essence of our body which is staying pious. The body remembers every touch and physical encounter it has had so it brings great discomfort if we are having multiple partners. *(Explained in chapter on sexuality)*

What happens if our romantic relationship doesn't last?

Sadly, this can lead to feelings of loneliness and emptiness, affecting self-esteem and self-worth. Additionally, it can create feelings of insecurity and fear of abandonment, making it more difficult to start new relationships.

Harmony can be created in romantic relationships. By understanding each other's needs, two people can adjust their behavior accordingly. A close bond can provide strength and comfort between two people.

How can one cope with a breakup?

After a breakup, a person may feel grief, sadness, and loss. There may be a feeling that they are not good enough, or that something is wrong with them. Breakups are traumatic. It can cause emotional and psychological trauma, including feelings of abandonment, rejection, loneliness, anxiety, depression, and anger.

Effects of trauma due to breakups:

- The person becomes introverted and stops reacting to things.
- Constantly thinks negatively.
- Extreme weight loss or gain.
- Constant restlessness, difficulty in sitting still.
- Speaking too loudly or too softly. Agitation of the mind and body (psychomotor agitation).
- Feeling tired or sluggish all the time.

- Constantly talking about the negative situation or not mentioning it at all.
- Feeling worthless or extreme guilt all the time.
- Mood swings are constant. One minute they're happy, the next they're crying.
- Not accepting the situation as it is.
- An inability to concentrate on anything.
- The loss of interest in almost everything. People are no longer excited about things that used to excite them.
- Eating too much or too little.
- Sleep loss or oversleeping.
- Constantly complaining about something.
- Experiencing feelings and emotions that are negative. Feelings of helplessness, betrayal, and anger are expressed.
- Experiencing extreme feelings like anxiety and fear.
- Anguish in the mind.
- The mind becomes dominated by negative emotions.
- Feelings of negativity resulting from negative thoughts.
- It affects self-respect, lowers self-esteem and self-compassion. Stress.
- Feelings of rejection and sadness.
- Avoiding social situations/running away from relatives and friends.
- Loss of will to live, self-destructive thoughts, recurring suicidal thoughts.

These are just examples and not the complete list of symptoms. Therefore, avoiding such situations is always advisable. Getting out of such situations can be difficult once they are too deep, and the consequences can be severe. A proactive approach to avoiding

such situations in the first place can also reduce the risk of being caught in such a situation.

Different forms of romantic relationships:

- **Marriage:** Typically, marriage is between a man and a woman. It is a legal and social union, usually recognized by society, in which generally one man and one woman make a commitment to each other to live together as a couple in an intimate and committed relationship. Marriage is seen to create a family and to provide for the raising of children. Commitment, trust, loyalty, and mutual respect are expected in marriage. It should be based on open and honest communication and sharing of feelings and emotions. A healthy relationship requires both spouses to be willing to make sacrifices and compromises. While dissolving it, a legal procedure must be followed.

  In some countries, same-sex marriage is legal. It is based on the idea that two people of the same sex can have a committed relationship and be just as valid as two people of the opposite sex. It is seen as a fundamental human right, and many countries have adopted laws to recognize same-sex marriages.

- **Live-in relationship:** Live-in-relationships do not have the same level of commitment as a marriage and are typically less formal. It is mostly based on physical intimacy. Sometimes, both partners may sign a simple written agreement which has no legal binding. These relationships are often more focused on the people involved and their individual desires, rather than on shared goals and expectations. In addition, physical intimacy is more prevalent in romantic relationships.

- **Romantic relationship:** The concept is based on a boyfriend-girlfriend relationship. In this kind of relationship, there

may or may not be physical intimacy. They prefer to stay at their respective homes. Eventually, this kind of relationship develops into a live-in relationship or marriage.

Despite not being a natural or blood relationship, marriage, live-in-relationship or romantic relationship is one of the most beautiful manifestations of evolution.

Relationships between partners have a lot of significance:

Any relationship is important, whether it is with a mother/father, a child, a sibling, a relative, a friend, or a colleague. We receive emotional support, joy, and love from our loved ones, but all these relations may not be able to provide the level of love and support we need. Perhaps there is a generation gap, or maybe they have issues that prevent them from being completely honest and reliable. These relationships are not available twenty-four hours a day, seven days a week. Our relationship with them is not permanent. We spend less time with family and friends than we do with our Partners (Soulmate, spouse, or boyfriend-girlfriend). So, our relationship with our Partner becomes more intense as a result.

What makes a partner's relationship different from any other relationship?

Several factors make these types of relationships unique and distinct from other types of relationships:

1. Social commitment.
2. The level of emotional intimacy.
3. Companionship and mutual support.
4. Shared long-term goals.
5. Physical and emotional Intimacy.

Advantages:

1. A lifelong partner provides a strong emotional support system. It is possible for couples to rely on each other during difficult times, which enhances their resilience and emotional well-being.

2. Sharing responsibilities: This type of relationship involves sharing household chores, parenting responsibilities, and financial obligations. Sharing responsibilities can result in a more efficient and harmonious life, easing everyone's burden.

3. A partner is a constant companion with whom to share life's joys, challenges, and experiences. Companionship brings happiness, companionship, and a sense of belonging.

4. Such relationships are a solid foundation for starting a family. Couples may have children through their union, allowing them to experience the joys and challenges of parenthood together. Despite the heterosexual partner dynamic, these advantages can be applied to any committed partnership, regardless of gender or legal status.

When making difficult decisions, having strong values and beliefs gives us clarity and guidance. Even under pressure, it is important to stay connected to own self and to our values.

Our intentions of getting married should be clear. It is a serious commitment and should be entered into with a clear understanding of both parties' expectations.

Section
2

Choosing a Perfect Symphony

1. Expectations from Partner

2. The Touch of Midas

3. Choosing a Partner

1

Expectations from Partners

An interesting discussion began between five young bachelors over a cup of coffee in a cosy and exclusive coffee shop. Topic? their expectations from a future spouse.

The first one says, "I want a beautiful wife."

"Like Aishwarya Rai?"

"No, not exactly. Madhuri dixit is also fine. Jokes apart, her figure should be captivating, fair, tall, and slender. I should feel proud to take her out with me."

The others agreed.

The first expectation had been finalized.

1st condition, 'Beautiful.'

The second friend said,

"My wife should be highly qualified."

"Why?"

"I have a high level of education. My intellectual hunger should be matched by hers. Likewise, our progeny will carry our genes forward. Genius is born this way."

All nodded in agreement.

2nd condition, 'Well Educated.'

Now it was the third bachelor's turn.

"It is not enough to have a good education. She should also have a good job. It is so hard to manage on one salary. Those days are long gone."

There was no doubt about it. All agreed. Naturally, salary was the subclause. Her high qualifications would mean she would be earning a handsome salary, which meant she must work in IT. Her job would require frequent foreign trips. Vacations could also be snuck in together with the husband.

3rd condition 'Good Salary Job.'

A little discomfort was evident on the fourth's face. There was things he needed to do around the house. As if on cue, he said, "My wife should have a good understanding of how to manage my house. I love to eat, rather, I live to eat. Therefore, she should be able to cook well. This makes women more hospitable. It's not the job of men. We have a continuous stream of guests. My mother has been performing her duties until now. The homely touch has been maintained. I want my wife to carry on the tradition."

How could they have missed such an important point? Everyone was surprised.

There was no argument or hesitation among them.

This concluded.

4th condition, 'Housekeeping Expert.'

As of now, the fifth one had not said anything. All of them thought that the story had ended.

"So, now we have our final list of expectations about the bride."

The fifth one was restless.

"Wait, we're missing something very important. Will she agree to take care of my parents if she has all these qualities? My parents have given up everything for my well-being, now it's my turn. My wife should take care of them. They deserve a few moments of contentment and rest."

"Bravo, that's a good thought. You're right," the first one said.

"I completely agree with you. She should dissolve in my house as sugar dissolves in water," said the second one.

"It's good that you thought of it. We were missing something important. She should be a connector of relations and not a breaker," the third one said.

"That's right. That's the last, but not the least, clause. She should love our parents as her own and consider our siblings as her own. She should take ahead our traditions, so well followed by our mothers. Of course! We are very cultured people. She should become one of us," fourth one concluded.

The five handsome bachelors agreed upon the fifth condition,
5th condition, 'Cultured, Loving, Looking After all In-laws'.

At this point, everyone was feeling relieved.

The discussion did not end here, however. They discussed the same for about an hour. For them, it was not fantasy, but reality. Because they weren't aware of their misconceptions about themselves, they didn't think their expectations were too unrealistic.

The last cup of coffee sealed the deal.

Each wanted to find his 'Dream Partner'.

With the idea of a wonderful choice of bride in mind, everyone was on cloud nine.

In the same coffee shop as these five 'would-be grooms' lost in daydreaming, a group of five young girls, 'soon-to-be brides', were also discussing the same topic.

The first said, "My house has rules. The words of my parents are final. After all, they know what's best for me. I did not object when my mother suggested that my name be enrolled in a matrimonial site. Why should I? Although sometimes I wonder if I really need to get married. My package is high. Since I am the only child, my parents' house will one day be mine. There are two cars in our family. I am greeted by my mother with hot snacks and tea when I return from work. My father manages my investments, bank accounts, and everything else. My life is so smooth, I wonder do I really need a husband?"

"Yes, you are right. My case is almost the same as yours. I don't want to get married. It's not worth getting into trouble. I am so happy with my life right now. If I do decide to marry, I don't agree with you leaving everything to my parents. It's our marriage, after all. How can they know what is good for us? Although I am not engaged yet, I know what type of husband I want in the future. I have prepared a list of expectations."

There was no disagreement on this point. Expectations were so natural! It was important for them to meet certain criteria in the guy with whom they were going to spend the rest of their lives. They decided to make a list of their expectations.

Now comes the first young lady with her list.

"Handsome, well-settled, an excellent package, cars, a bungalow, or at least a spacious flat, not many responsibilities, these are the basic expectations."

"I agree, but I will say 'no responsibilities at all.' Do we have the time for them?"

"Yes, that's right. It is better for me to be part of a nuclear family. I have seen some of my friends. After working tirelessly in the office, they have to deal with household duties. It's just impossible for me to stand near the kitchen platform. I am not a good cook. We can either have a cook or pack lunches and dinners. After a long and tiring day at work, I have the right to relax and enjoy a readymade dinner. It won't just be my husband who is privileged. If he expects me to care for his parents, what about mine? My parents have worked as hard to raise me as his parents. The groom's parents should not be the only ones considered. Let me tell you something! In my family, I want a sweet, caring, genuine person who will dissolve like sugar. I expect him to respect and love my parents and brother as if they were his own."

"How is this possible? It is not in our tradition."

"Why not! Forget about traditions. I am highly qualified, earning a good salary. My parents have a spacious flat. He will have to stay with my parents. I am not willing to stay with my in-laws. My mother has a knack of understanding me. Will my mother-in-law have it? When I return from office at 8 p.m., will she be able to serve me food as my mother does?"

"It will be so nice if we can stay with our parents after marriage."

In the midst of fantastic thoughts and a cup of coffee, they finalized their list.

It was a cloud nine moment for five beautiful girls.

● ● ●

Finally, the second 'would-be groom' and the fourth 'would-be bride' were married.

In all aspects, they matched extremely well.

However....

Despite tremendous tensions, misunderstandings, distress, and many 'missed' aspects, the couple got divorced after two years.

There is no guarantee that every marriage will go through the same hell, but it is possible.

•••

What do you think of these expressions?

Boys:

- "I work like a donkey throughout the day. I expect a cup of tea and some fresh and hot snacks from my smiling wife." (Conveniently forgetting that his wife also works for long hours.)

- "My mother looks after everything the whole day. My wife should take charge of the kitchen at night." (Wow, what a high standard of expectations.)

- "My clothes and socks and hankies and toiletries…. My better half should keep everything organized while I get ready for my office. I don't much understand these things." (How convenient!)

- "Actually, it is my Partner's job to take care of my things and that of the household things as well. Females are better at this. The house should always be presentable." (Shooting someone after putting a gun on their shoulder.)

- "I like it when my wife cooks dishes, especially when she serves it fresh and steaming hot." (Wow, how could he possibly not enjoy this?)

- "My mother needs to visit the doctor today. My wife should take leave."

- "Our children have a holiday today; their mother should also manage a leave."

Wow, wow, and wow again.

An image of a perfect traditional marriage.

●●●

Girls:

- "I return home bone-tired. At least thrice a week, my husband should keep tea ready for me." (Is it too much to ask?)
- "I want to appoint a cook. I will also enjoy dinner with my husband when I return from the office. And yes, at weekends, we will go for an outing. I will not cook at all." (Is it healthy eating?)
- "A yearly tour to somewhere out of India is must."
- "Shopping and movies are essential, rather they are my oxygen. How can I otherwise survive in this mundane job and more mundane life?" (Your oxygen should be a sound, happy relationship.)
- "I don't want to take a chance of pregnancy for the first two-three years at least. I need time to get adjusted to the new situation." (Isn't it the decision of both partners?)
- "I need a house-keeper, a gardener and a chauffeur as well. And yes, I need a separate car too." (No problem if it comes from your income.)

●●●

Analysis of the story:

The boys are still in traditional marriages, and the girls have already moved on from it.

The expectations of both teams were too materialistic. However, none expressed a desire to have a Partner with a positive

attitude, an honest mind, respect for others, and a sense of respect for self.

It was all about "HOW CAN 'I' BE HAPPY!" Too engrossed in fantasy and assumptions!

Why do I want to get married? What is the purpose of my life? Is marriage going to help me achieve it? Will I achieve self-actualization? Will I follow the path of progress? Have I ever considered staying 'together'? Is companionship really something I am aware of? Body-mind-soul congruence: what does it really mean?

Prior to plotting expectations about the Partner, no attempt was made to answer these questions. If they had found answers, their perception of a Partner would have been different.

'Being together' is the foundation of these questions. It is not wrong to wish for our Partner to understand us. It is also important to recognize that this is a two-way process. Each Partner must understand, care for, and balance the other. It is only then that togetherness blesses both parties. It should be a win-win situation for both the partners. Alternatively, we can live a life full of compromises without being willing to make them.

It is only when both Partners are willing to connect on all levels that they will experience a blissful life. Families, parents, and souls would enjoy a wonderful life together.

It is natural and rational that we expect a Partner who is compatible with us, and there is nothing wrong with that. But do we really know what compatibility is?

Also, it is obvious to want to spend time with someone who is cheerful, educated, well-mannered, cultured, and civilized. Before

expecting this from someone, there is a need to see whether we possess these qualities.

Is it wrong to have expectations?

No, you're taking a wrong turn. It is quite right to have expectations. We all have expectations from our partner. Whether it is an arranged marriage or a love marriage, there will be expectations. But it is important that these expectations should be realistic and rational.

Our five handsome boys' expectations 'Good Looking', 'Highly Educated', 'Highly Paid', 'Expert in Housekeeping', and 'Cultured' girl. On the other hand, young girls sought: A handsome boy, well-settled, good package, a bungalow-at least a spacious flat, no responsibility. Wow, this is a great choice. The combination of beauty and brain is unbeatable. And when she matches other expectations too, it is unquestionable that every bachelor would desire such a bride, and every likely bride would prefer such a groom.

A case study of beauty expectation:

Radhika was a beautiful girl when she started living with Ram. Four years was a very heavenly experience. And one day she had an accident. She survived with traces of many scars on her face. Her life changed drastically because of the scars that made her look ugly. Her confidence and zest for life diminished. She was no longer the same beautiful girl she once was. After this tragic incident, Ram left her. As if by magic, Tanay entered her life as a lifeline. His support turned this ugly duckling into a swan. She overcame her insecurities and moved on. Through accepting her flaws and loving herself unconditionally, she learned to accept

herself. Now, she has become stronger and more resilient. Her return took two years. She learned a lot about life in these two years. Ram regretted his behavior after seeing her after two years. Despite his apology, she never accepted him back. Tanay and Radhika married and now live together happily.

From the perspective of a counsellor:

- She learned to accept herself as she was by accepting her flaws and loving herself unconditionally. She has become stronger and more flexible as a result.

- It took her two years to complete her journey. During these two years, she learned a lot about life.

- After seeing her after two years, Rama regretted what he had done.

- Despite his apology, she did not accept him back. Radhika and Tanay are married and living a happy life together.

A case study of well-educated expectations:

Arun is a brilliant young self-employed man. He dropped out of school at a young age. After barely passing class 9, Arun started driving a rickshaw to support his family. Everyone appreciated his behavior. He is forty years old today. Despite not having a degree, he speaks excellent English and helps everyone. Since his partner loves to learn, he has enabled her education up to the MA level. Now he would like her to do a PhD. His children have been taught good manners by him. He owns five rickshaws and rents out ten cars. Because he has a cultured manner, he talks and walks like a highly educated man even though he has no formal

education. So, can we say, he doesn't have education, but he has wisdom?

From the perspective of a counsellor:

- He has excellent emotional skills.
- When he visits, he says, "Doctor, I have stopped learning."
- Then I say, "You have learned a lot without learning. Can you tell me anyone who called you rustic or uneducated? If you want a degree, you can get it at any time."

A case study of a good salary expectation:

There was a young couple named Roopa and Swaroop. Both were employed. They had a daughter. Roopa decided that she should quit her job and take care of the baby until she turned seven. When she informed Swaroop of her decision. He refused to accept this. If Roopa didn't do a job, so she wouldn't be paid. He was going to lose all the money he had planned on having for the next few years. He told her not to leave her job. She became angry and said, "Who are you to tell me that? For my daughter, I will take the decision."

Both remained firm in their positions. There was a fight. There were arguments and no conclusions. They both lost the joy of having a beautiful daughter. Roopa was under a lot of stress. As a result, her milk dried up. The two rushed to the counsellor.

From the perspective of a counsellor:

- The desire for Roopa to raise her daughter is very natural.
- There is financial pressure on Swaroop. This is also fine.
- It will be up to them to decide this question by speaking with one another.
- They should come to a joint decision.

A case study of housekeeping expert expectation:

Sarah, a dedicated career woman, juggled the demands of her job with grace and determination. Yet, as the days blurred into nights, she found herself shouldering the burden of household responsibilities alone. David, her loving husband, was no stranger to hard work, but his contributions to domestic duties were sporadic at best, confined to occasional gestures rather than consistent efforts.

As the weeks turned into months, the strain of their unequal division of labour began to take its toll on their relationship. Sarah felt overwhelmed and exhausted, while David struggled to understand the depth of her frustration. It was during this discord that a quiet realization dawned upon him – he needed to step up and share the load.

With newfound determination, David approached Sarah one evening, his heart heavy with apology and resolve. He confessed his oversight and pledged to become a more active partner in their shared life. Sarah, surprised yet hopeful, welcomed his sincerity with open arms, eager to see where this newfound commitment would lead.

And so, their journey towards equality began. David started small, taking on simple tasks like washing dishes and folding laundry. Though unfamiliar at first, he embraced each chore with determination and dedication, determined to prove his love through action rather than words alone.

As days turned into weeks, David's efforts blossomed into a true partnership. He learned to cook simple meals, clean the house with care, and even master the art of grocery shopping. With each task completed, he felt a sense

of pride and fulfilment, knowing that his contributions were easing the burden on Sarah's shoulders.

But it was not just the physical tasks that strengthened their bond – it was the intangible moments of connection that truly transformed their relationship. As they worked side by side in the kitchen, laughter filled the air as they shared stories and dreams. They discovered that the true beauty of partnership lay not in the division of labour, but in the shared joy of building a life together.

As time passed, Sarah and David's home became a sanctuary of love and equality, where each task was a testament to their commitment to one another. Their journey was not without its challenges, but through patience, communication, and unwavering love, they forged a bond that was stronger than ever before.

And so, in the heart of a bustling city, amidst the ebb and flow of daily life, Sarah and David danced to the rhythm of their love.

From a perspective of a counsellor:

- Their relationship was forged not only through physical exertion, but also through the moments they spent working together. As they worked in the kitchen, they told jokes to each other and shared their dreams. Their bond was strengthened not just by sharing chores, but by the joy they got from working together.

- Sarah and David's home gradually became one of love and equality where every task symbolized their commitment to each other.

- Harmony, tolerance, and never-ending love made their journey pleasant, despite the challenges they faced.
- They formed a strong bond that had never existed before. In such a tidal flow, Sarah and David danced to the rhythm of their love.

A case study of looking after all in-laws' expectations:

Take the example of Maya and Raj. Their story was a tapestry woven with threads of tradition, love, and duty. But within the sacred circle of their union lay a commitment that transcended the bounds of matrimony, the care of their aging in-laws.

Both Maya's and Raj's parents were treated equally in their home, Maya's parents enjoyed the privileges Raj's parents enjoyed. Both parents had access to the same resources, including fun opportunities, healthcare, and financial support. They were treated with respect, and their opinions were equally valued.

Raj and Maya always say, "We are blessed with two mothers and two fathers."

From a perspective of a counsellor:

- Raj and Maya always say, we have two mothers and two fathers.
- Both spouses have a rule of gender equality in their homes.

For ages, married couples have walked in the same direction. Are the expectations mentioned above incorrect? Does that mean we shouldn't have any expectations?

As times have changed, what was relevant to that era is no longer relevant. We need to alter our expectations. To make our life together blissful, we must understand that these expectations

are superficial. Are we overlooking something vital? These expectations were mostly general. It was a continuation of worn-out thoughts. Coexistence and cooperation were less prevalent. Most of the time, it was a one-sided affair.

Before plotting expectations every person should question, "Do I possess the qualities I expect from my Partner? The question is of, "Am I complementary to my partner's expectations?"

Every thought stopped at 'What Do I Want?' 'Is there anything I can give?' was never in the near vicinity. There was a lot of talk about 'Me' and 'Mine' in terms of expectations and criteria. The word 'We' had no place.

The rules of the games have changed, but the young men are not ready to acknowledge them. They never seemed to be touched by equality. The girls, on the other hand, were becoming aware of their hopes, aspirations, and identities. In realizing that they too have expectations, they began to express them. So, we need to carefully plot our expectations when we expect 'Rhythmical relationships'.

In a rhythmical relationship, two hearts move in perfect harmony, creating a symphony of love and connection. A strong sense of joy, peace, and contentment often accompany the feeling. Two people are in sync when they are both physically, mentally, and energetically in sync. The feeling is one of completeness.

2

The Touch of Midas

The touch of Midas transforms ordinary objects into shimmering gold, evoking awe, and wonder. Beauty and abundance are endless when the mundane becomes extraordinary. In the same way, when we find the right Partner in our lives, our lives become more meaningful and more beautiful than we ever imagined. We feel complete and joyous when we are with our Partner. It's like the touch of Midas. As soon as our partner touches our lives, we should feel an unexplainable connection.

The choice of partner:

The choice of a Partner should not be based on chance but rather on wisdom.

We know that 1 and 1 = 2, but we can change this equation to 1 and 1 = 11. Wrong selection would never allow us to accomplish this as it can lead to resentment and conflict. The journey of two would become towing or dragging. Self-actualization would remain a fantasy. Living together can be a hellish experience if not handled properly. Breakups are often traumatic, both emotionally and financially. There are a lot of legal processes, energy and time

involved. It would be a big mistake to be casual. We cannot deny the importance of choosing the right partner for us.

How do you specify who is the right partner for us?

The selection of a Partner is not a game of chance. However, it is a matter of choice. Our greatest milestone in life is living in harmony with our partner. Therefore, selecting a partner is a thoughtful process. When it comes to choosing the right partner for us, generally the answer is, who is compatible with me? The answer I will give is a bit different. With fifty years of marriage and many years of marital counseling under my belt, I have a different definition of the right partner.

"A person with good values, beliefs, morals, who is well educated and has a background of culture. A wise person who treats others with dignity and equality. A person who is ready to grow and will help others to grow."

A culture of respect and mutual understanding can be fostered by surrounding ourselves with such individuals. Building a strong and peaceful relationship requires such qualities. It creates harmony, peace, connection and create meaningful exchange.

Please note,

When I say, a well-educated person, it does not necessarily mean a university degree, but rather, I mean the type of education discussed in the last chapter.

It's up to the individual to decide what other factors are important to them, such as compatibility, education, beauty, career, housekeeping, salary, and so on. The choice is totally up to the individual. Even though compatibility is a personal choice, we shouldn't reject it.

Three colour light: traffic light?

When choosing a partner, let's use the three-coloured lamp. Like traffic lights, these lights have three colours. In other words, it is a way for you to determine what qualities you are looking for in your partner. It is up to each person to decide what qualities to list in a colour lamp.

Listed below are a few examples:

- **Green coloured light: Partner must have these qualities.**

It is essential and necessary for the Partner to have a positive and optimistic outlook on life. EQ is high. He/she should be flexible, assertive, but not stubborn. Successful marriages require such qualities. If you want a partner who possesses the same hobbies, likes and dislikes, add such items in this list.

- **Yellow coloured light: Essential but not necessary, may have or may not have.**

A give-and-take relationship, loyalty, trust, commitment, gender equality, partner's liberalism, and belief in equality. He/she should be prepared to participate in housework. The partner should be compatible. A strong foundation and a long-term marriage require such qualities.

- **Red coloured light: Should not have these qualities.**

Among the harmful qualities are a tendency to torture, addictions, personality disorders, a high level of ego, etc. These and other vices should be recognized and avoided if present.

Everyone should make their own list based on their preferences.

Let's understand what is compatibility:

The concept of compatibility refers to the ability of two or more entities to work together to achieve a common goal.

Compatibility refers to how well these two entities can cooperate, collaborate, and coexist. Successful Partnerships and collaborations require compatibility. It is the feeling of being one, with sound communication and harmony. The presence of compatibility can lead to successful collaboration, which in turn can lead to better results.

Those who are compatible tend to have similar values, interests, and habits and enjoy the same activities. Often, they can work together to achieve their common goals and values. Couples who share similar interests are more likely to be on the same page, understand each other better, and have fewer disagreements in their relationships.

Living under the same roof makes it difficult for two people to stay continuously happy twenty-four by seven with or without compatibility. It can be difficult to identify compatibility if the two do not match. At such a time, it is imperative to communicate effectively and recognize the differences between the two. A compatible relationship can be fostered by bridging the gap between the persons. In many aspects, two different people will have different opinions. There is nothing erroneous about it. Couples can also be compatible if they do not match. How is this possible?

The compatibility aspect of a relationship changes as it matures. There is usually a lot of compatibility immediately after marriage. Incompatible issues are often ignored by newlyweds or 'newly-in-love' couples. It is generally the motto 'Aim to Please' that motivates them to make the other happier and merrier. Despite not liking the activity, she goes on a trek with him, and he sees a movie of her choice.

Compatibility in various fields

Let us see what these fields are:

1. Psychological makeup.
2. Personality types
3. Aspects of physical health
4. Emotional world
5. Social aspects
6. Relationships
7. Education/IQ
8. Locus of control
9. Defense mechanism
10. Problem solving
11. Attitude
12. Outlook towards life
13. Finance/economics/money
14. Spirituality
15. Work culture
16. Communication
17. Physical Intimacy
18. Cultural Differences
19. Lifestyle
20. Conflict Resolution
21. Morality
22. Values and Beliefs
23. Life Skills

The following three fields are important to evaluate a partner's compatibility:

1. **Morality:** Morality is more objective and fixed than values, which can change over time. To build trust and respect in a relationship, couples should strive to have the same moral code. By discussing and agreeing on shared values, as well as actively listening to each other's opinions, this can be accomplished. But the partner should understand that morality can be subjective, and two people may have different moral views that can still be respected.

2. **Values and beliefs:** Life values are the principles and beliefs that guide our actions and decisions, shaping our character and defining what is important to us. They provide a moral compass and help us navigate through the complexities of life, ensuring that we stay true to ourselves and live a meaningful

existence. Values can be both subjective and objective, and they can be shaped by our life experiences and beliefs. It is important to take the time to consider our values and evaluate if they are in line with our goals and values. There are many important life values and it will be different for each one of us. Here are some general important life values such as integrity, respect, empathy and kindness towards others, responsibility, tenacity, gratitude, forgiveness, unconditional love, being self-reliant. It is preferable for couples to share the same values and beliefs. They can walk happily together on a path of togetherness by using life values. Important life-values for Partners are the following:

- **Integrity and honesty:** Being honest and open with each other builds trust and strengthens relationships. Establishing a strong bond between individuals requires integrity and honesty. An open and transparent relationship develops a sense of security and reliability, fostering a long-term and healthy relationship.

- **Respectful Behavior:** It is important to treat each other with respect, both in private and in public. Respect and acknowledge each other's individuality, opinions, and boundaries. When we respect others, we foster a harmonious and inclusive environment where everyone feels valued and heard. It encourages open-mindedness and empathy towards different viewpoints while promoting healthy relationships.

- **A belief in equality and the right to equal opportunity:** For a relationship to be successful, both Partners must contribute equally and make decisions together. When they are equally involved in decision-making and take responsibility for

their actions, mutual respect and understanding are fostered promoting mutual respect and understanding, which allows people to trust each other and work together towards a common goal. The concept of equality also encourages both partners to feel valued and supported, allowing them to express themselves freely without fear of judgement.

When both partners are given equal opportunities to contribute and make decisions, a sense of empowerment is fostered, and a balanced distribution of power is encouraged.

- **Empathy:** Compassionately and with understanding recognize our Partner's feelings, thoughts, and experiences. Be there for them in times of need and support their endeavours. Being empathic allows us to truly understand and relate to our Partner's emotions and perspectives, allowing us to provide genuine support and be a comforting presence during their challenging times. It is giving our Partner the assurance that they are not alone.

- **Commitment:** Both Partners should be committed to making the relationship work, nurturing it, and investing time and effort into it. They must be open and honest with each other, express their feelings, and support each other's goals. It also means resolving conflicts peacefully and quickly. As a final point, both Partners should be willing to compromise and work through any issues that may arise.

- **Having faith in individuality**: Supporting each other's goals and aspirations while respecting each other's independence. Relationships should allow for personal growth and individuality. Unconditional support should be provided. Our relationship will flourish if we respect our Partner's decisions.

- **Being forgiving and accepting:** Everyone makes mistakes, and conflicts are inevitable. For happy living, forgiveness and acceptance are essential. Accepting each other's flaws and forgiving each other's mistakes, allowing room for growth and learning is a wise thing to do. Trust and respect can be built through forgiveness, while understanding and bonding can be strengthened through acceptance. We can form stronger relationships with each other. It makes a world of difference when we are together.

  The list can go on. Together, couples should decide what values or beliefs they want in their relationship.

3. **Life skills:** To build a strong foundation for a relationship, couples need life skills. The ability to adapt and positively respond to the demands and challenges of daily life is referred to as a life skill. Life skills based education, according to UNICEF, is a behaviour change or behaviour development approach that addresses knowledge, attitudes, and skills. They apply across the lifespan and promote and protect life, health, and well-being in risky situations. A person's life skills include psychosocial competencies and interpersonal skills, which assist them in making informed decisions, solving problems, thinking critically and creatively, communicating effectively, building healthy relationships, empathizing with others, and managing their lives effectively.

List of important life-skills

1.	Adaptability and flexibility	4.	Decision-making skills
2.	Communication skills	5.	Critical thinking skills
3.	Problem-solving skills	6.	Time management skills

7. Stress management skills
8. Financial management skills
9. Self-awareness and emotional intelligence
10. Networking and relationship-building skills
11. Leadership skills
12. Conflict resolution skills
13. Active listening skills
14. Goal setting and planning skills
15. Resilience and perseverance
16. Negotiation skills
17. Creativity and innovation
18. Assertiveness and self-confidence
19. Digital literacy and technology skills
20. Mindfulness and self-care skills

There is no end to the list. Consider how ambitious we are when we expect our personality to match our partner's. It is important to remember that everyone is different and has their own unique set of interests, regardless of age, profession, gender, or culture. The importance of being open to different perspectives and ideas cannot be overstated. Together, couples should decide what values or beliefs they want in their relationship. What is most important is the willingness to learn whatever is necessary.

Degrees and levels of compatibility:

Couples may have compatibility in many areas, but degree and level of compatibility may differ when partners pursue them at different levels.

For example:

- *Shree and Soha accepted their differences also understood compatibility they have. They are living a happy life by sharing similar interests and goals.*

- *Both likes movies but he likes crime movies, while she prefers romantic movies.*
- *It is common for both to eat outside food on a regular basis. His frequency is once a week, while hers is once a month.*
- *Both may want to reduce pollution, but one may be more concerned with short-term solutions while the other may be more concerned with long-term solutions.*
- *Both like travelling, but one likes sea beaches, and the other likes snow-clad mountain trips. One may like travelling once or twice a year, the other may want to go every two months.*
- *Both partners may have a sweet tooth, but one likes only bakery products and the other may like traditional sweets.*
- *Both may like reading but one may read fiction and the other likes Outlook, Money and Reader's Digest.*
- *Both may enjoy outdoor activities but one may love horse riding, golf or polo or badminton and the other may simply want to go for a picnic to relax.*
- *Both may like driving but one may want only to drive safe distances and for work purpose and the other may like taking long road trips.*
- *Both partners may like non-vegetarian food but one may prefer only sea food and the other poultry.*
- *Both may like going to meet friends occasionally but one may like planned visits and the other may make impromptu plans.*

Handling compatibility differences:

- Understanding and accepting that our Partner and we are different is essential. Make a note of it that despite many areas where we are similar, we are going to be different.

- First and foremost, we must accept that we are different. Rejecting its existence will not reduce the problem, rather, it will intensify it.

- Identify the areas where we have the same opinions and make them more concrete. When these areas are found together, they also reveal non-compatibility areas.

- Understanding each other's family views, cultural differences, and religious beliefs; political views, experiences, maturity, etc. is a smart move.

- When there is a difference of opinion, don't blame it on not being compatible. Even couples without hurdles as mentioned above occasionally have disagreements, such as how to spend their vacation, where to dine, when to visit relatives, etc. Embrace differences and agree to disagree. Never try to change the religious or political views of someone else.

- Respect one another's opinions, value each other's experiences. It is the foundation of any relationship.

- We have discussed this point before, but we will reiterate it once again. It is more important to find similarity in life-values than compatibility in personality.

Remember these points:

1. The other party is also looking for fulfilment of their expectations from their Partners. If we do not meet them, we will be rejected.

2. Identifying harmful points such as extremely high ego, addiction, personality disorders, outrageous tendencies, etc., should not be avoided or, at least, should be given serious consideration.

3. If you were looking for the perfect bride/groom, would you marry yourself? I find it interesting to ponder over this question before plotting expectations.

4. Do you possess the qualities you seek in a partner? Assess your own qualities and see if they match those you are looking for in a partner. If not, consider how you can improve these qualities. By having them, you'll be in a better position to find the right partner.

Consider the following:

Every individual has the right to live their life as they see fit. Dreams and aspirations, thoughts about life, blueprints have all been made by each of us. A Partner's ideas and notions match our own, which makes the journey ahead easier. Otherwise, when the couple's aspirations clash, one of them needs to take a step back to avoid negative consequences and then either or both Partners must let go of their dreams after marriage. This is a heartbreaking situation for both. The two can be equally happy if they understand each other and adjust. This can be avoided before a relationship begins with a solid living together or live-in-relationship foundation. Each Partner must be clear about their dreams and decide how far to modify their dreams or how far to step back to allow the other to go ahead. Continuous compromise from one Partner is a disaster for both partners. Communicating feelings requires honesty and openness from both partners. Compromise is necessary, but it should be based on mutual respect and understanding. Compromise is impossible without open and honest communication.

Let us consider this example:

One Partner	Other Partner
Loves pets, wants to have a mini animal kingdom.	Fears animals, rather hates them.
Loves various forms of arts.	Has no interest in arts at all.
Likes to travel, spends a lot on moving around the world.	Hates to travel or to spend on it.
Very strong stand on ethics and values.	Quite flexible about ethics and values.

This list is endless. Initially, these seem like trivial issues, but they are the root causes of long-term and long-lasting disputes. Taking precautions before is an excellent idea.

Does this mean that couples with different dreams shouldn't get married? That's not what I mean. The love between the Partners allows them to accept each other's dreams and to let go of some of their own. Surely life together should be fairly portrayed. They may both be happy if they do it. Each party should contribute and compromise, it should not be one-sided. It is important that both parties strive to create an atmosphere of mutual understanding and respect. To achieve happiness, they should also remember that they are equals.

Adjustment is a right and a choice each of us has, so if both partners are reasonable, they will surely adjust and then accept.

They might say to each other, "If I don't like it, that's okay. You can go ahead. In any way I can, I will support you. I am always there besides you."

Beware of factors causing trouble

- **Addictions or Dangerous Habits:** There are a number of dangerous habits that should not be ignored, such as substance abuse and physical abuse. Substance abuse includes addiction to drugs, alcohol, and other substances which affects physical health issues, mental health issues, and legal issues. In addition, it can increase the risk of accidents and social isolation. Physical abuse results in damage to a person's and partner's physical and mental health. In addition, long-term trauma and difficulties forming healthy relationships can result. An individual who has been physically abused may become anxious, depressed, and mistrustful of others as a result. Low self-esteem, difficulty in concentrating, and difficulty forming healthy relationships are also possible consequences. Physical abuse can also cause long-term health problems due to physical injuries. These habits can irritate the Partner if things continue in the same way over a period.

- **Mental diseases:** Mental disorders include schizophrenia, borderline personality disorder, bipolar disorder, narcissistic personality disorder, dementia, Alzheimer's disease, depression, and anxiety and many more. Such disorders may be hidden by a partner, or they may not be exhibited in a short period of time.

- **Physical diseases:** Heart disease, TB, AIDS, and many other health problems are dangerous. It is impossible to know about them unless you are specifically told.

Here is an example of how she made a wise choice in selecting her partner.

Neeta was a very smart, talented, and highly educated girl from a rich family. She earned a great salary. She was aware that she wasn't good-looking, maybe a little less than average. A matrimonial site suggested Ramesh's name. For some reason not known to her, she wasn't comfortable with the information given. Despite her reluctance, she agreed to the meeting. It was Ramesh and his parents who came. She felt uncomfortable throughout the meeting. After the guests left, she told her parents,

"I'm sure they'll say no. There is a lot of smartness and beauty in the family. Why will they approve of me as their daughter-in-law? I am no match with respect to beauty."

As a matter of fact, the exact opposite happened. Neeta was chosen by the handsome and good-looking family.

"Tell them I'm not ready for this relationship," Neeta declared.

The shock on her parents' faces was apparent. Ramesh was well liked by them.

"The salary he earned was good, a little less than Neeta's but that's okay. What a handsome boy!" They thought.

Neeta, however, was not convinced. Realistically and rationally, she asked, "What was it about me that they liked?"

Her mother answered, "You are smart and intelligent."

"I would have liked it a lot if they had really done that. It was fun talking to Ramesh. He could be a good friend. But unfortunately, while talking to them, I realized that the

family was overall very handsome and the most important part is that they are aware of it. His mother is so beautiful. I think the only criteria they considered was my salary."

"How can you say such a thing?"

He mentioned it to me. He said, 'I liked you, it was my mom's opinion that you looked inferior. But I insisted.'"

There was silence from the parents.

Neeta continued, "Mom, I was surprised, where had they seen me before? So, I asked him. He said, 'In the photo.'"

Neeta's voice was clear and filled with hurt.

"When a person feels that I am inferior to him, I would not be willing to give my life to him. This inferior-superior concept bothers me. Marriage should not be viewed as a competition. What if tomorrow I wish to quit my job and sit at home looking after home and family? I will again be considered inferior by him or they will object to this decision."

Mom had no answer.

"Baba, his mother asked me if I could cook. All of them are foodies, she said. There is no doubt that she is an expert cook. That's not all. The man said he wanted to take a loan from the bank showing my salary slip to buy a big house, so I had to give him my pay slip."

"Man?"

"Ramesh."

"What did you say?"

"I asked for his pay stub, he was shocked, and he refused."

"...."

"They want a bride who'll work more, earn more. Rather than a beautiful bride, they chose someone like me who isn't even attractive, but makes a lot of money. Why?"

A murmur escaped her lips.

"As an only child of wealthy parents, I have an added qualification for them."

Their daughter's foresight impressed both parents.

From a perspective of a counsellor:

- Neeta took a decision keeping her eyes and ears open.
- Moreover, her habit of thinking in detail came in handy here.
- She saved herself from making her future life difficult.
- Choosing a partner wisely requires paying attention to many factors.

Find a partner with whom sharing similar values and interests is possible and this is crucial to building a life together. Couples should also have a strong emotional connection and be able to trust one another.

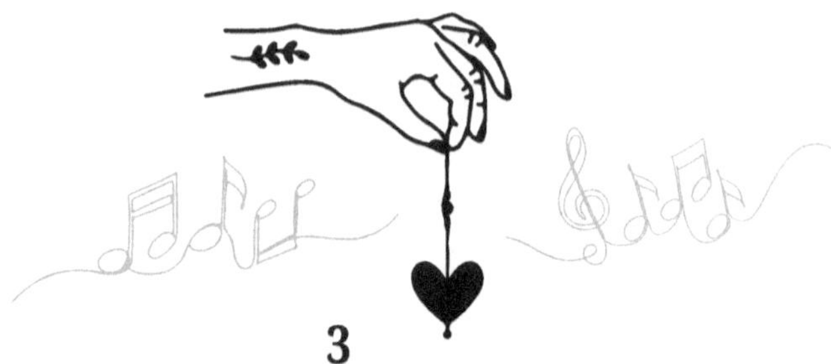

3

Choosing a Partner

Choosing the perfect Partner is a fantasy. This idea lies in our heads. Our dream is always to find a romantic, flawless partner. But in reality, no one is perfect or flawless, so we should focus on looking for someone right for us. It is more likely that we will select a decent and good partner, if we outline some important traits based on our psychological make-up.

Partner selection for a love marriage, a romantic relationship, or a live-in-relationship

'I saw, I liked, I fell in love, he/she is my soul mate, I want to marry and live happily ever after.'

This story is a fairy tale.

An intense and immediate attraction to someone is love at first sight. Usually, love at first sight is based on physical attraction or perceived similarity. There is nothing like matured love at first sight to ignite a spark between two people. Matured love or true love which is required for long-lasting relationship goes beyond initial attraction and requires effort,

Since our childhood, we have been inspired by romantic love stories like, Heer-Ranjha, Shirin-Farhad, Romeo-Juliet etc. It is

our dream to find our own prince/princess charming/beautiful and true love.

Living together begins with a romantic feeling. With the hope that this can lead to a deeper connection and relationship, people start living together. Often, they believe that living together can help them build trust and intimacy, as well as strengthen their bond through shared experiences.

Choosing a partner for an arranged marriage

In this case the Partner is selected after a thorough investigation. It is often helpful to learn from the experience of parents. In the beginning, we try to identify a person's educational, social, physical, economic status and family background. We seek the help from our families, friends, relatives, social networks, people at the person's office, and marriage bureaus. In this process, parents and/or elderly relatives guide the process, so it is likely that there are similarities in the families on various aspects, such as education, cultural aspects, economic status, language, living-style, food habits and many more things. 'Life together' may become easier and more flexible. As parents play an important role in finding a partner, they will naturally offer support if needed. As an example: managing the family affairs if the daughter-in-law has a job or business, raising grandchildren, etc. Many times, we use the latest technology, such as apps, e-mail, chatting, etc. The Internet has brought the world closer together. It is possible to interact with people who are far away through chat, e-mail, virtual meetings, etc.

In marriage, finding a suitable partner, marriage rituals, shopping, lavish dinners and lunches, first night, honeymoon, all these events are wonderful and can bring a lot of joy and

excitement. We dream of being loved and cherished and living a happy life. Our hope is to find someone who will understand us and be our romantic partner throughout our lives. With this idea in mind, we decide to get married.

Warning bells

We begin our relationship with romanticism, and then we get bitten by the bug. There are warning bells. Despite our best efforts, life does not move as we had hoped. Eventually, we realize that life is not a fairy tale and that our dreams are unattainable. Our romantic love begins to fade as we become disillusioned with life. To find our true purpose, we must face reality. The flame cannot be kept alive by romantic moments alone, as living together or marrying is a long-term commitment. With the help of a partner of our own choosing, we should be able to transform romantic love into mature love. Lifelong bonds are always our goal.

It is the time to evaluate our selected partner

The partner has been selected. What's next?

When we meet someone, we fall in love. We may feel a connection with them and want to spend the rest of our lives with them. There are times when we go against our families or even the world to grab the love of our lives. We are mistakenly convinced that our choice does not need a second thought. It is possible that we will not realize the consequences of our actions until it is too late.

After selection of partners, it's just 'me and my partner' chilling in a romantic relationship. It is like being in seventh heaven. Promises are exchanged. It is a competition between each other to please our partner. Dreams and hopes are shared between them. The boy is ready to bring the moon and stars for the girl. The girl blushes when she sees the boy. With their romantic togetherness,

they create a world where love knows no bounds and dreams seem a reality. Their hearts are intertwined, painting a picture of a future filled with endless love and shared experiences. They smile at one another without reason. They see the world as pink and blue. It's all shiny with silver linings, no difficulty or pain.

Even when they receive red signals, they tend to ignore them, even when they are obvious. Cognitive biases lead people to believe that bad things will never happen to them, or that they will be able to avoid bad outcomes.

Everything is rosy for them; they live in their own bubble. Both believe that this bond will last forever. No matter what happens, they promise to stay together. With a kiss, they promise to remain true to each other. There is no doubt in their minds that they can make it last forever. They seem to be on cloud nine, where everything is perfect and blissful. The only thing that remains unsurpassed is joy and happiness.

If it is a marriage, families of the bride and groom are busy shopping, buying gifts, planning lavish ceremonies, and arranging various events. Following that is the wedding day and then the honeymoon. The story of living together does not end here, rather it begins. We are still unaware of the difficulties and realities of living together. It can be challenging due to conflicts in sharing responsibilities and personal space, as well as differences in lifestyles and communication styles. Navigating and overcoming these challenges requires open-mindedness, compromise, and effective communication.

We can follow some steps:

1. We should reflect on our decisions and think about whether we have selected the right partner. Can I spend the rest of my

life with this person? To find answers to these questions we should take the time to get to know this person we selected and determine whether we share the same values, beliefs, and goals.

2.   We need to discuss our future with our partner and see if we're ready to accept each other unconditionally.

3.   If either partner feels they have made a wrong choice, then it is time to rethink the selection. It is better late than never. It is not necessary to carry wrong decisions throughout our lives. Corrections can be made at any time, but it is best to do so as soon as possible.

Generally, there is a tendency to hide negative aspects. During courtship, very few people reveal their true faces. People tend to present themselves in the best possible light when courting someone. A person who is interested in them tries to demonstrate that they are desirable, capable, and worthy of the other person's love.

How can we find out whether our selected partner has the qualities we expect?

Don't worry, even after selecting our partner, we can still win. We can find out the facts before starting a relationship. Courtship period is the best period to know many things. We should use this time to get to know each other personally, so that we can build a strong and lasting relationship.

- To better support each other in the future, we should discuss our individual goals and expectations.
- Let's get to know each other's families.
- Understanding each other's backgrounds, compatibility, values and beliefs, life skills.
- Understanding emotional competence, locus of control, defence mechanism.

- Understand each other's perspectives and way of thinking.
- Information like education, culture, financial status, job, etc.
- Family dynamics.
- Previous affairs.
- Strange habits.
- Mental issues such as borderline personality disorder, bipolar disorder, substance abuse disorder.
- Physical issues that are not visible unless they are disclosed.

The list is not complete. There is a possibility that the other person will not answer honestly. Ultimately, he or she would give desirable answers.

Here are some examples:

"Do you drink alcohol?"

"I don't."

It is possible that the person answering does not consider social drinking to be drinking.

●●●

"Are you prone to anger?"

"No, I am not a short-tempered person."

●●●

"Do you like shopping?"

"I spend thoughtfully."

●●●

"Do you believe in values and ideals?"

"Yes, I have very high values."

●●●

"Do you accept bribes?"

"What the hell! I am the 'cleanest' person in my office."

●●●

"Will your mother ill-treat your wife?"

"Not at all, she is the most loving person."

•••

How do we get the right information?

For the same, there are four methods.

1. Direct communication
2. Observation
3. Psychological tests
4. Exchange of files with true certificates
5. Appointing a private detective

1. Direct communication-

Meeting each other as often as possible is essential. Meeting places and times should vary. All important aspects should be discussed during such meetings. Love language, career aspects, likes and dislikes, aims and goals, reason for getting married, economic stability, running the home, ambitions, division of labor, childbearing age and number of children, life ideas etc. The most important condition is that answers should be sincere and honest. Along with the physical and mental aspects, financial status should not be ignored. To confirm the income, pay slip should be verified. Of course, this information cannot be demanded in the initial stage but it can be seen at a later stage. Rather, before the other person demands it, one should willingly share the details if everything is going well.

There is a questionnaire which can be used to gain pertinent information. Meetings are a good time to ask these questions. This can be done tactfully during casual conversation so that the other person does not know what information is being extracted.

Questions to be asked for getting information about partner:

Questions to in-laws:

Childhood is the root of many problems, and it is where many habits are formed. It is important to understand the dynamics of your partner's family. And for this best, the way is to meet the parents of your partner.

Let's go on a date with the in-laws. Discuss each other's families, how they raised their children, and how they view the world. Discuss your partner's values and beliefs and how they have helped to shape them. Communicate honestly and openly. There should be two-way communication. If we tell them about ourselves first, they won't feel like we're digging for information. Our childhood and family dynamics should also be known to them.

Questions should be asked casually and it should be in such a way that we can learn more about the partner's family background and interests. We can share our own values and beliefs and ask theirs. We can agree to follow up on the conversation with more visits and interactions in the future.

For example:

A girl asked her mother-in-law how she pacifies her son when he is angry, a brilliant question. The mother-in-law smiled and said, "I've learned that listening to him and acknowledging his feelings go a long way. I try to understand his perspective and find a compromise that satisfies both of us. The key is to create a safe space where he can express his emotions and come up with a solution together."

Or she may say,

"He becomes calm on his own when I leave him alone without asking any questions."

His anger pattern will be revealed by this question.

Here are some examples of questions. It is up to you to formulate your questions based on what you feel you should know about your partner.

Some examples:

1. "I'm sure my mother has many funny memories of me. Telling these is her favourite pastime. Can you recall something funny about ...... as a child?" You can take it a step further. "What about you, Aunty? You must have been quite a child. Do you recall any of your childhood events?"

2. "Aunty, I love watching movies. I like family drama. Do you?" If she says yes, then, "Great we can watch together. And your son?"

3. "Could you share some good childhood memories of your daughter/son?"

4. "Painting is my heart, it's not my hobby, it's my breath. Do you have any hobbies?" Slowly, ask her about her son's hobby and what it means to him.

5. "Was he/she naughty? Honestly, I was very naughty. The teachers always punished me, but with time I became a milder version of myself."

Family traditions, cultures and values:

Tradition, culture and values are areas of disagreement between partners. Differences in upbringing, personal values, and exposure to diverse perspectives can lead to disagreements on tradition and culture. Finding common ground and compromising can be challenging when both partners hold deeply ingrained beliefs and practices. At such times, it is wise to be open to compromise and adjust one's own beliefs while recognizing and respecting the other person's values and beliefs. To maintain a healthy relationship, it

is important to find a middle ground that satisfies both partners. Thus, it is important to know some information about this field before entering into a relationship.

For example:

By skilfully asking and sharing our family dynamics with our in-laws, we can create a better understanding of our relationships. Our feelings and needs can also be expressed in a respectful and constructive manner.

You can say,

"On Sundays or on holidays, my father cooks, and give my mother a complete holiday. Sometimes brother joins hands with him in preparations. All ladies of the house get the entire day off. Or they both order food from outside, and my father insists that the food must be of my mother's choice. My mother prepares and serves what we like on all other days. She must have her turn one day." The benefits of a break for a mother must be weighed against the long-term effects on children's perceptions of gender roles and expectations.

"Aunty, if you like this idea we can work together on this program and tell all the guys to manage on Sundays. What do you say?"

In a tactful manner, we can ask the following questions indirectly. Also, we can ask questions that encourage them to think about the issue and come to their own conclusions. To encourage the other person to speak, we can use body language and facial expressions to signal our interest in the response. We can also ask open-ended questions to give the other person a chance to elaborate.

1. *What are some of the most important family traditions or customs in your family?*
2. *How do you celebrate festivals?*
3. *In your family, how do you celebrate holidays and special occasions?*
4. *What values or beliefs are particularly important in your family?*
5. *What is the cultural background and heritage of your family?*
6. *Does your family practice any cultural practices or rituals that have been passed down through generations?*
7. *What is the impact of your family's cultural background on your daughter/son's upbringing?*

Relationships within family:

Having an understanding of family relationships is important before getting married. It can help identify potential issues and provide insight into how your family may respond to your marriage. Having a better understanding of your family dynamics can also lead to stronger bonds and healthier relationships. Make sure you include topics that are important to you.

For example:

"Laxmi Pujan is a big event in my house. Every family member and friend is invited to take prasad. We chat and play games all night long. Early in the morning, we enjoy tea together and disperse. It's so much fun. We all wait for the whole year for this occasion."

Or

"We call our friends to celebrate every small event."

"Whenever possible, we prefer to spend festivals and birthdays with our close family members."

Questions to be asked to the Partner before marriage, to understand partner well.

These questions shouldn't be directly asked. After sharing our information, we expect our partner to respond.

Personal Background:

1. *How did you grow up and what is your family background?*

2. *Do you have any significant experiences or events that have influenced you to become who you are today?*

3. *My closest among family members is my sister, who I can always count on. In times of need, I know I can rely on her. For advice and comfort, I turn to her. Who is the person with whom you are most closely connected?*

We can cover all the areas we consider important in a similar manner. It is impossible to know everything before you start. Getting into a relationship will bring many surprises, but we are taking precautions to avoid failures. Different communication styles, conflicting expectations, and discovering new aspects of your partner's personality over time can create surprises and challenges in relationships. Even though it's impossible to know everything beforehand, taking precautions such as open and honest communication can minimize the risk of failure and help navigate these surprises.

Surprises bring joy, excitement and freshness in relationships. They have the ability to strengthen the bond between partners by creating moments of love. These surprises keep the relationship fresh and dynamic.

2. **Observation-**

   After meeting with a partner, careful observation is necessary.

- Appearance, way of dressing, body-language, eye movement, tone and way of talking, any habits, communication style with the waiter or any such person (servants at home), parents, relatives.

- Keen observation of the house along with the household appliances and décor also tells a lot about the person.

- The behaviour of family members with each other reveals family dynamics. Family culture, way of treating the women of the family, social and economic status, educational background, etc. can be understood by observation. One should make it a point to see old family photographs. This would also give some idea about the family. Family's ideas about spending vacations, recreation and leisure time tells a lot about their hobbies. Exercise patterns, reading newspapers, etc. seem to be trivial aspects, yet they are very important.

- Eating habits are another vital issue. Preference for vegetarian food or non-veg, junk food consumption, smoking/drinking habits, playing games/sports, dominating nature, self-centeredness (as per latest research self-centered people have less self-control) are various important aspects.

- Visiting his/her workplace would give an idea about his/her way of working, treating colleagues, etc.

3. **Scientifically proven tests-**

   Some people may or may not provide correct information about their physical and mental health. They may misguide us by projecting something else than what they really are. Hence, getting tests done will be the best approach. Complete physical and mental

check-up, family medical history, life expectancy ratio, ailments if any, etc. should be tested.

4. Information Sharing through file-

The Partner may also disclose a file of his/her personal details honestly and willingly if one partner expresses a desire and sincerely asks for it. There is no problem with preparing one file and giving it to the other party. All the details about us can be shared this way, such as the ailments or diseases that family members or we have suffered; especially physical and mental ailments, educational and achievement certificates, a call-letter from the current organization where we work, a pay slip, and physical medical reports (blood, sugar, ECG, etc.), salary slips, close relations list, and other things which we have told them about us. This proves our trustworthiness. By providing this information, we demonstrate our willingness to trust the other person to make the right decision. As a result, we exhibit our integrity and commitment to the truth. We can ensure that others have all the information they need about us by doing this. If we reveal first the Partner will be encouraged to speak freely and share his/her file with us.

The more we tell our partner about our likes and dislikes, ideas, prospects, motivation, aims, nature, etc., the more our partner will follow in our footsteps. It may be difficult for some people to speak freely. We will have to demand the personal file if it is not handed over to us. That doesn't mean we have to be rude. It is more effective to be pleasant than to be harsh.

5. Arranging a private detective-

Private detectives will gather information about potential partners. The purpose of this method is to get information about potential partners by conducting a thorough investigation and

learn more about them. Private detectives are reliable sources of information that can't easily be obtained through other means.

Important Tips:

Now we come to the last, but not the least, aspect. It is a revolutionary idea. It is a custom that the bride goes to stay with the bridegroom after marriage. The necessity of these times is that both should go and stay at each other's homes prior to marriage. A weekly stay would give a fair idea about the family in detail. This will help to take decisions more correctly. This is specifically applicable in a joint family. Though this may sound absurd, today it is the need of the time. We are not suggesting that 'both would-be' should stay under the same roof without anyone around, rather it is the other way around. They should be surrounded by family members. This indeed is an idea worth considering.

It is time to take the actual decision now. It is a fact that in whatever way the 'marriage-knot' is tied, there will be plus and minus points. Even after taking all precautions, our partner's behaviour may still surprise us. Keeping an open mind and being willing to forgive mistakes are important. It is important to accept and understand our partner's perspective. We should be willing to compromise and work together to resolve the issue.

Don't be afraid to disclose your decision if your mind is steady and firm.

Congratulations, it's the right decision you have made. Take responsibility for your decision. Red roses are waiting for you. Make sure you hold your partner's hand tightly.

Section

3

Creating Harmony

1

Lighthouse Fundamentals

We can create our own unique sound, share our dreams, and support each other in our creative endeavours when we work together. We can learn and grow together. We can create meaningful moments together by creating our own music. But don't forget that the road to success is a little slippery.

Getting to success can be a little slippery

There are many unexpected twists and turns in this story. It requires perseverance, resilience, and adaptability to overcome the challenges that can come our way. One moment we may be cruising along smoothly, and the next we may encounter obstacles or setbacks that make us stumble. Keeping focused on our goals, learning from failures, and pushing forward is the key. The rewards and satisfaction of reaching our destination make every step worth it.

A partnership with fruitful and successful living together do not happen overnight. It needs to be cultivated and fostered. Everyone wishes, 'My family should be a one-of-its' kind with lots

of understanding and love.' But how many of us are willing to put in the required and honest efforts for this? Rather, how many of us are aware that we need to work hard towards achieving this? In any relationship spontaneity, naturality, wholesomeness does not develop automatically. A 'Happy family' is neither the result of sheer luck or chance nor of careful selection of the partner or a self-proclaimed state. A carefully and thoughtfully selected, intelligent, good-looking partner does not ensure a happy married life. One needs to put in sincere and honest efforts to make the marriage happy and successful.

What does it mean when we say, 'One needs to put in sincere and honest efforts?'

It means:

- Being prepared to sacrifice
- Adapting to people as they are
- Adapting to the environment
- Accepting and taking care of change
- Accepting commitment and responsibility
- We should be willing to acquire required skills and qualities even if we do not possess them.

There are many other things to consider and accept as well

- Many skills like strength, intelligence, managing emotions, willpower, and determination to maintain relationships are necessary.
- Partners need to give time for development of emotional and physical intimacy, attachment, and commitment.
- Close friendship needs to be developed between the partners.

- Respect for each other and enjoying staying together in harmony will cultivate such friendship. Partners must learn to enjoy small things in each other's company.
- The more the partners know each other's dreams, likes, dislikes, strengths, and weaknesses, the more an intimate friendship will be developed.

This process might initially appear to be tedious, complicated and time consuming, but if the emotional and social intelligence of the partners is well developed, it may not be that difficult. The feelings of sacrifice, understanding and acceptance it involves, give satisfaction. Moreover, the fruits one reaps after implementing this in day-to-day life makes one forget about its complexities.

The rate of success in married life increases when some fundamentals are followed. Success, may it be in career or in living together, is like a lighthouse. It guides us in the right direction.

Seven Lighthouse fundamentals:

The best way to believe in the utility and importance of these fundamentals is to try them out and see the results. There are ten of them. Think about them, try them and only then, practise them.

They are,

1. Respect your Partner's opinion.
2. Avoid labelling your partner.
3. Understanding your Partner
4. Staying together, staying tuned to each other.
5. Emotions are contagious (Mirror neurons).
6. Use of a pause button, don't react, respond.
7. My partner and I are two separate entities.

1. Respecting your Partner's Opinion:

Every person may have a different opinion on every issue. Basically, everyone thinks in his own unique way and develops a different approach or perception. Hence, no opinion is right or wrong. That is why before rejecting the other's opinion, we need to think about it, and we should respect their opinion.

For example, there are some people who prefer to go on romantic dates to the seashore, while others prefer to go on romantic dates to the mountains. A candlelight dinner or a garden dinner may be more appealing to some.

The couple should agree that decisions will be taken after considering both opinions. For example, how to spend the bonus money awarded to either the husband or wife should be decided by both. The approach of 'I will spend as I please' should not be adopted. In living together, 'you' and 'I' do not exist as separate identities, but rather as a team. The responsibilities of both the partners are shared rather than individual. Even small differences of opinion will result in swords drawn if this is not accepted.

Keep these things in mind:

- Neither partner has to be right or wrong.
- Different opinions should not be resolved solely by logic or arguments. There is also an emotional component to this that needs to be addressed.
- Consider your partner's opinion and understand their reasoning.
- It is important that both partners consider what is best for their team rather than what is best for their individual interests.

2. Avoid labelling your partner:

Different people are labeled differently by us. Once we label, it becomes our favorite game to prove that we are right. We fail to recognize the other person's viewpoint. These labels then become the standards or barometers to gauge their expressions and behaviour. Our mentality of "labelling people" will disappear if we change our approach. 'Always' and 'never' are the words for labelling.

"He is always saying 'No' for everything."
"She is always the first one to start the fight."
"She never tries to compromise, it's always me who does."

3. Understanding the Partner:

In any relationship, understanding our partner is crucial. By being open and honest, we will be able to build a stronger bond and create a lasting relationship. There are differences between us as well as similarities. It is then easy to adjust, accept and adapt to differences. Until they both change their attitudes, they will not be able to develop a deep relationship; rather, they will remain at a superficial level. Empathy and active listening are essential to understand a partner effectively. Understanding the other's perspective enhances the emotional quotient.

4. Staying together, staying tuned to each other:

Tuning is essential for a pleasant lifelong journey. We need to walk aligned with our partner, if we want to be together forever. Strength, depth, and expanse are more important in a relationship than speed. Furthermore, walking together develops cohesion. To achieve family happiness, it is essential to strike a balance between the personal enjoyment of each family member and the happiness

of the family. If we understand that happiness for each member of the family equals happiness for the family, many twists and turns in relationships can be eliminated. We will surely contribute positively to this goal.

5. Emotions are Contagious (Mirror Neurons):

It is contagious to smile. When you smile, it spreads like wildfire. An angry face leads to many angry faces. This happens because of 'Mirror Neurons' present in the human brain.

A person's emotions can be mimicked by onlookers using these 'Mirror Neurons'. When a person talks to someone lovingly, then they are bound to respond in the same way, they can feel the emotion of love. 'Elements of Purity' are love, peace, sanctity, happiness, knowledge, and power. That is why we should surround ourselves with people who are loving, smiling, and positive. They represent positive energy. Through a 'Mirror Neuron', someone experiencing these elements of purity in their hearts will also demonstrate positive behavior. Having even one happy and positive member in the family will lift the mood of everyone else.

The things one can do,

- Every morning, wish your partner 'Good morning' with a smile and a big hug, regardless of what happened the night before. Your partner feels warm and happy when he receives it. A strong bond creates a sense of connection. The positive mood it sets for the day is also a great way to start the day.

- A light joke shared over breakfast will create a lighter atmosphere. It will also help break the ice between partners and start conversations. It can also lighten the mood and make the day more enjoyable.

- While leaving for work, wishing your partner is a great idea.
- During lunch break call the partner and ask, "Have you had your lunch?" Brilliant act!
- The next time your partner returns home, connect with him/her saying "Are you tired? Your favorite coffee is ready." This shows him/her that you care about him/her. You can also show support by massaging his/her shoulders. You can build trust and strengthen your relationship by talking to him/her and showing him/her you care.
- When your partner is experiencing negative emotions, acknowledge their feelings but don't make negative remarks or comments. Respond with positive emotions only. Reassure them that you are there to listen and to help. If you are not asked for advice, do not give it.

6. Use of the pause button, don't react, respond:

As soon as an incident occurs, our midbrain takes a decision and activates the system. We are not able to respond in our natural way. The reaction is given automatically, which means that our thoughts have no control over it.

But we forget that our brain has a capacity to avoid such reactions. By considering our long-term needs and goals, we can provide a correct response. Pushing the 'Pause' button will allow us to do this. Instead of reacting, let's respond. Rather than getting carried away by emotions, let us think about the outcome and have a clear vision. We should respond through our behavior based on our deeply ingrained values instead of an thoughtless impulsive reaction. We will then be able to enjoy a comfortable life with our partner, all we need to do is hit the pause button.

The pause button can be used between incidents and responses. Nature has given mankind this very valuable gift. Because of this gift, we have the freedom to think in our own way. It will be our response after the pause, that determines whether it will benefit us or harm us.

The pause button can be used in a simple manner. Count one to ten or take three consecutive deep breaths before answering. Our higher brain will have time to analyse, and our mid-brain will not have an instant emotional reaction.

Counting numbers from one to ten has been taught to us since childhood to control strong emotions. Anger can be controlled with this simple trick. Scientific evidence supports this claim. The 'Six Seconds' trick can make wonders because anger to control and then compassion to develop takes just six seconds.

7.   Me and my partner are two separate entities:

The two of us are separate entities. Our backgrounds, interests, and goals are different. Our experiences and perspectives are different because we are two different people coming from varied backgrounds. These differences are what make us unique and special. Our Partners may have different opinions, thinking styles, behaviours, values, and beliefs than our own. There will be a difference in the psychological make-up of our partner. The assumption that my partner will be the same as me will lead to misunderstandings and conflict.

To avoid conflicts these differences should be embraced and used to build a strong, loving relationship. Finding a balance between honouring our differences and being united as a couple is

crucial. By learning about each other's backgrounds and cultures, we can appreciate the unique strengths each of our perspectives brings.

Despite our differences, we complement each other and offer unique perspectives. Our diversity allows us to grow together and learn from one another, strengthening our bond.

The unique perspectives and strengths of each other are valued and supported.

To build stronger, more meaningful relationships, it is more important to accept our Partners as they are and value them.

We can reach a resolution that is satisfactory to both of us, if we find common ground.
Building a strong, healthy, and fulfilling relationship, requires understanding our partner. Communication, connection, trust, respect, and the ability, to navigate life's ups and downs are fostered by it.

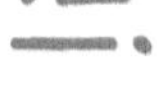

2

Melodious tunes

Friends hold a special place in everyone's life without a doubt. As a counsellor, I am referring to friendly traits that bring joy, harmony, and melody into our lives together. These are:

1. Positive thinking and optimism.
2. Emotional and social competence.
3. Forgiveness.
4. Quality world.
5. Unity of thoughts.
6. Adjustment, acceptance, and adaptability.

1. Positive thinking and optimism

Optimism and positive thinking have scientifically proven advantages that are well established.

People who are optimistic are more motivated to improve themselves and reach their goals. The optimistic person sets goals that stretch their abilities and succeeds in accomplishing things they previously thought impossible.

2. Emotional and Social Competence

What is Emotional Competence? (EC)

Being one of the most positive and useful skills, EC helps us to understand our feelings and emotions in a better way making

it easy to name them accurately. This enables us to fathom their intensity and appropriately handle them. The best part is that EC empowers us to reach our aim without struggling along the path.

Peter Salovey and John Mayer first introduced the concept of emotional EC in their paper 'Emotional Intelligence'. Today, it is a proven fact that EC is more important than IQ. Our success, happiness and contentment are based on our emotional relations with others, be it our workplace, business, social life or any other area. It is true that intelligence helps us to conquer success in a materialistic way, but emotions allow us to stay connected with people. Our happiness depends upon this connection.

Some people are basically soft, mild, and mature. They accept the feelings and emotions of others as well. As they are balanced, they do not end up judging people wrongly or with a prejudiced mind. Not all are balanced. There are many who must struggle a lot to control their thoughts and emotions. They are unable to accept and handle others' emotions. Forget anger and grief, they have no control over their happiness as well. Their EC is quite low hence it becomes difficult for them to manage their relations, social life, and workplace atmosphere.

How can one improve Social Competence?

The most essential part at this stage is understanding the emotions of others first.

- When we meet someone, we must try and understand their emotions and feelings.
- Secondly, observe their overall language, tone, and body language, as these act as a thermometer. This makes it possible to understand them well.

- Maintaining a fair account via a personal diary would prove to be an excellent aid. We generally express ourselves honestly in a diary. It also helps in catharsis. It allows us to fathom the depth of our emotions.
- Self-talk.
- Active listening.
- Empathetic approach.
- In case of differences, avoiding crossing the third stage of conflict and developing the skill of staying calm.

3. Forgiveness

The act of asking for forgiveness and forgiving is not a sign of weakness, rather it is an indication of self-confidence in the person asking for forgiveness. Anger and hatred, on the other hand, are signs of weakness. Despite going something wrong or making a mistake, remember that mistakes are only a few pages in the book of life. You do not have to discard the entire book if you need to tear that one page.

When we make a mistake or when we hurt our partner, usually we just say sorry and move on. But saying sorry isn't enough. Saying 'sorry', means we are expressing our sadness or feeling bad, but what about the person who was hurt? You must be forgiven by your partner. Saying sorry should be followed by forgiveness from the partner; that will be the real resolution.

It is best to say, 'I'm sorry, please forgive me'.

Here, two words are used: 'Sorry' and 'Forgive me'.

Sorry: This word indicates that we regret our actions or words.

Forgive me: We are asking the partner to forgive us, to give us another chance, to understand our mistake.

Our hurt partner will realize that our intention was not bad if we ask for forgiveness immediately after a mistake. Then he/she can decide whether to forgive us. If our partner forgives us, the hurtful words or actions are more likely to be erased from both minds.

If someone asks for forgiveness wholeheartedly, it is best to forgive them. Asking for forgiveness and forgiving is a science as well as art.

4. Quality world

Deep within our minds, we perceive a world and therein lies a quality world. It is like an album wherein pictures of ideas and ideals, things and people are stored securely. In our mind, we see the world from our perspective. We acknowledge it from the ideas we get. This creates an image in our mind. The world is just the same, be it you or me. The only thing that makes it different is our perspective. Hence, we all have our own special and perceived world which becomes our 'Quality world'. What do we include in it? The things which we think will enhance our living and existence. These may include our house, family members, relatives, hobbies, travelogues, places we wish to visit, our spiritual and religious expectations and understandings, etc. Each quality world is unique.

5. Unity of thoughts

When both partners are united in their thoughts, a successful and happy togetherness can be achieved.

Communication and collaboration require unity of thought. Achieving success becomes easier when both partners are on the same page. It is important that both understand the purpose and objectives of the task clearly and concisely. When embarking on a journey together, it's like having a map; if we don't have the same

destination in mind, we'll get lost. Maintaining an open dialogue with regular conversations can help us stay on the same page. Building trust can be achieved by creating a more collaborative and productive work environment.

Take the following example: When Ram and Sita decided to get married, one thought lingered in their minds. If we don't get along, what will happen?

The two decided that, "We will always be together. Separation will never be an option for us. No matter what happens, we promise to stay together. We vow to always be open and honest with each other. No matter what obstacles life threw at us, we are confident that we will overcome them."

This unity of thought made it possible for them to live together happily. They often struggled with their differences but found ways to remain happy together. By working together, they realized their differences could be a source of strength. They would transform their insecurities into strengths. Their mutual respect and understanding led to a sense of purpose and unity.

6. Adjustment, acceptance, and adaptability

The three steps to a healthy relationship with a spouse are adjustment, acceptance, and adaptation. Here is an explanation of each step:

- **Adjustment:** Adjusting to accommodate each other's needs, preferences, and differences is essential in any relationship, including a marriage. Compromise and finding common ground are key to this. Communication styles, lifestyle choices, and decision-making processes can all be adjusted. Healthy relationships require a willingness to adapt and change.

- **Acceptance:** After adjustments are done, the need is to accept your partner as they are, including their strengths, weaknesses, and imperfections. Embracing their individuality requires letting go of unrealistic expectations. By accepting your spouse, you foster a sense of trust and security in your relationship.

- **Adaptability:** After acceptance, the next step is adaptation. It refers to the ability to evolve as a couple in response to life changes, challenges, and growth. Relationships are dynamic, and circumstances and individuals change over time. It is essential to adapt to these changes, making necessary adjustments to ensure that the relationship remains strong and resilient. New circumstances may require modifying roles, priorities, and goals.

As we are together, we are playing snakes and ladder. Whether we climb a ladder or get eaten by a snake depends on our actions. The rules of the game are determined by our actions. By doing good deeds, we move up in rank and reach our goals more quickly. Conversely, if we do bad things, we are punished and must work our way back up.

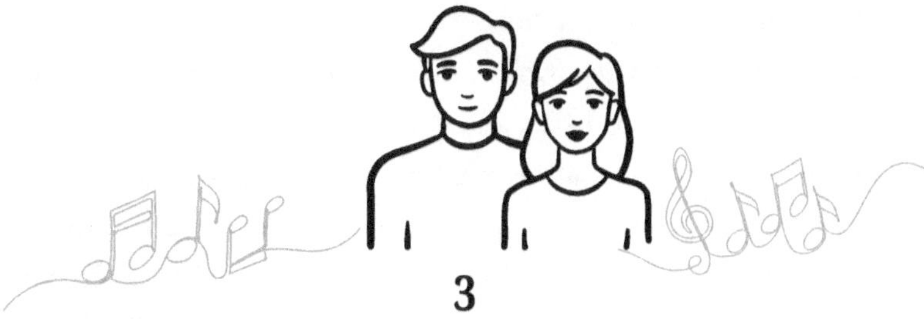

3

Women and Men are Different

Women and men differ biologically, genetically, socially, and culturally in many ways.

When we are talking about living together, we will talk about biological and genetic marginalization. Social and cultural differences are not acceptable to us. We will be able to adjust to one another better, if we accept the biological and genetic differences between women and men.

Men and women are two separate elements, and there is no inferiority or superiority between them. No one has a senior position, and the other a junior position. The status of women and men should be equal. For this union to be harmonious, both partners must work hard and put equal effort into it.

There will always be genetic and biological differences, but if we can overcome this, we might be able to achieve rhythmic relations between partners. This can be achieved by taking pride in the women's and men's roles (femininity or masculinity), and accepting them gracefully and respectfully.

The social and cultural differences between men and women need to be addressed.

The differences will go far beyond these few.

- Women are often disadvantaged in terms of access to resources, economic opportunities, and decision-making positions.
- It is expected that after marriage, the wife will live at her husband's house. A wife is expected to adopt the traditions/cultures of her husband's family. It is expected that she will carry forward the same traditions/culture, no matter how different they are. What is the reason for this? Because traditions/culture created by society say so. Her failure to do so will be seen as disrespectful and uncaring.
- She may also be held responsible for any misunderstandings or disagreements between her family and her husband's family.
- He can give his parents money for their monthly expenses; however, if she wants to give some money to her parents, why does she need permission from her husband or her in-laws? No matter how financially independent she is, her husband or in-laws would be the ones to make all financial decisions for her. She could be viewed as violating her marriage contract if she gives her parents money without their knowledge.
- Even if she works the same hours as her husband, it is expected that women will do household chores.
- Women are expected to prioritize housework and childcare over work. Rather than pursuing a career, it is seen as a way for society to ensure that women's primary role is to care for their families and children.

What can we do to overcome this difference?

It is important for men to recognize the importance of gender equality and strive to create a more equitable environment for

women. And it is their responsibility to understand and resolve these differences.

- Both partners should decide where to live after marriage. Firstly, with his parents. Secondly, at her parents' house. Or a third option is that the couple should move to a separate house. It is ultimately up to the couple to decide which option is best for them.

- Both his parents and her parents should be treated equally. Taking into account the dynamics of the family, the couple should come to an agreement that works for them. They should discuss their expectations for the future and how they plan to manage their finances. Lastly, they should reach an equitable and fair agreement.

- It is only fair that her parents receive the same privileges as his parents. She should not ask permission from her husband or in-laws if she gives some money to her parents for monthly expenses, for example. It should be up to her to make a decision.

- In this way, the couple will be able to create a financial plan tailored to their specific needs and circumstances and will remain on the same page. As a result, both parents will feel respected and treated fairly, and their children will benefit from both parents' sacrifices and hard work.

- Is it a wonderful thing if she could create a tradition amalgamating her traditions/culture and her husband's traditions/culture, creating a more open and modern traditions/culture. Creating an atmosphere of understanding and acceptance could help to unite both families. As well as strengthening family ties, it can create a sense of belonging for the couple.

- When it comes to house chores, both partners should contribute equally. This will create a sense of responsibility and fairness in the relationship, as well as ensure that neither partner is overwhelmed by the amount of work to be done. As both parties work toward the same goal, it will also help create an atmosphere of unity and cooperation in the relationship.
- She should take decisions regarding herself. When it comes to her, she has a right to make her own choice.

Trust and understanding can be strengthened when both partners work towards the same goal. Both parties can feel respected and valued, resulting in better communication and smoother decision-making.

Biological and genetic differences:

It will be always very beneficial for us to understand how the biological traits differ between men and women, and how their conduct, thoughts, feelings, emotions, awareness and manifestation are different. If we think that though we are different from each other, we complement each other, then, this relationship can work wonders. When we accept this distinction consciously and willingly, then the chances of love will increase much more, and a tuneful relationship will be created in both of them.

Benefits:

- There can be a lot of progress in the company of each other and both will be very happy.
- Tolerance is going to increase.
- A healthy relationship is built.
- Having a better understanding of our partner will help us to work together more effectively.

What are the biological and genetic differences between men and women?

There are three aspects:

1. Emotions
2. Thoughts.
3. Behaviour (actions)

These three different qualities of men and women can be classified into nine aspects:

1. Physical formation and skills.
2. Thought process and emotional make-up.
3. Needs and expectations.
4. Goals and their priorities.
5. Conversation style, methods of interacting with others.
6. Reaction and conflict resolution methods.
7. To handle differences and problem-solving methods.
8. The way to live and work in life.
9. Relationships.

The following explanation will tell us how women and men are poles apart from each other:

Men and women differ in many respects. Biological, physical, psychological, and social differences separate men and women in the following ways:

1. Physical formation and skills.
2. Thought process and emotional make-up.
3. Needs and expectations.
4. Goals and their priorities.
5. Conversation style, methods of interacting with others.

6. Reaction and conflict resolution methods: 'Handling differences and problem-solving methods.

7. The way to live and work in life.

8. Relationship.

Please note:

- It is important to note that these differences are generalizations and do not apply to everyone.

- These differences do not imply superiority or inferiority of one gender over another. Women and men have unique strengths and abilities that contribute to their overall cognitive function.

- Individuals should be treated and respected as unique entities rather than being solely defined by their gender, as there is considerable variation within each gender.

However, both men and women share many similarities. Women and men value financial security. Both men and women can achieve success in any field they choose.

Although men and women have different appearances and functions, they are inextricably linked and dependent on each other.

For Example:

Once a humorous seeker told me, "Doctor, I only remember one thing you mentioned about men and women. If my partner behaves differently from me or not the way I want, I say to myself, 'He is a man. He will behave differently from me,' then I don't get angry with him."

I couldn't stop laughing.

"Girl, your technique is very cool. And suppose your mother-in-law behaves differently?"

"So, I say to myself, 'As the doctor said, not everyone will act the way I like because everyone is different.'"

This girl has used her self-talk very effectively.

I just told her, "Bravo!"

Women live on Venus and men live on Mars. Women are often seen as the planet of nurture and love, whereas men are seen as the planet of aggression and competition.

4

Communication

"Good communication is a bridge between confusion and clarity,"
Nat Turner.

Let's understand what communication is:

The ability of an individual to be able to covey his or her thoughts, views, and feelings to another individual or a group of individuals is called communication. It is a doorway of expression that enables an exchange of what is going on in our minds.

As they say, practice what you preach, so we must learn more about communication and bring it to use in our lives with our partners, children, family members, colleagues, friends and develop better relationships in every sphere of our lives.

What is the need for Communication?

Communication is one of the biggest needs of current times. To be able to express ourselves to others and to be able to understand what they want to say meaningfully it is crucial that we learn the art of communication.

The following are the main needs of communication:

1. **To inform:** communication is highly required to inform one another about what is going on in our mind. When we know how to communicate effectively, we can make the other person understand what we want and how we want it. Improper conveyance of information in various situations can lead to conflicts and misunderstandings that, at times, cannot be rectified or cause great discomfort when trying to be resolved. Especially when we talk about relationships, it is important that we keep each other well informed of our needs. In both personal and professional areas, a well- informed situation is better than any misunderstanding arising due to lack of information. In relationships, it is important that both the partners understand the importance of informing each other about decisions, thoughts and required details so that both can make a base for a fulfilling relation.

2. **To express feelings and emotions:** communication is needed to be able to express our feelings and emotions when we are working on ourselves, our relations with others, family members, friends and other spheres of life. Our feelings and emotions make up who we are and thus must never be suppressed. There could be times when the desired situation needs clear expression of how we feel. Hiding feelings and emotions or not expressing them is a reason many couples drift apart. We cannot assume that the other person will understand our feelings and emotions miraculously and will perform his or her actions so that we are not hurt, but once we develop the art of communicating ourselves, we will be able to avoid such misunderstandings.

3. **To be straight forward:** the art of communication needs to be straightforward and not go round and round a topic. We should be able to say clearly how we think, feel or wish about a particular situation instead of hiding or saying misleading things. The other person becomes insensitive to or takes it for granted when we do not express ourselves as we want to. No one likes to be told one thing once and another thing a second time in a similar situation. Being clear and precise is better than feeling the hurt later.

4. **To have empathy:** Communication skills promote empathy towards the Partner which helps in understanding what the Partner is feeling and the thoughts and behaviour underlying these feelings. It helps to establish the relationship on strong ground and clarify problems.

Types of communication:

There are various ways in which we can communicate with everyone around us. It is widely seen that people use words to express themselves and those who cannot speak use sign language to be able to be understood. In current times, more and more people are realising that it is important to be heard not only via the usage of words and language but also to have clarity. Various types of communication are explained in detail. These are:

1. Verbal communication
2. Non-verbal communications

1. Verbal Communication

Verbal communication includes communication that shows a desire to comprehend or discuss what is important to the other person, here it is the Partner. In this method, we use spoken or

written words to convey our feelings, ideas, beliefs, information etc. across to the other person. When words come out of our mouth, i.e., when we are speaking, our voice, tone, and other things like pauses due to breathing are considered. This type of communication is most suitable in humans as they can speak and listen, respond and understand easily through vocal communication.

We can further categorise verbal communications in two groups. These are:

- Active Verbal Communication
- Vocal communication.

Active Verbal Communication:

This includes several ways of directly responding to a Partner's messages such as greeting the Partner, confrontation or using a humorous response. Some of these are discussed below:

Greeting each other early morning when you start your day, wishing each other at night and even speaking with softness in telephonic conversations is active verbal communication. The expression is conveyed clearly, precisely and concisely and the effect can be seen instantly with a smile and a positive response returned from the other Partner.

A person's vocal messages can speak volumes about how emotionally responsive they are to the other's feelings. The following are five dimensions of vocal messages which can be remembered in the form of an acronym **VAPER**:

- **Volume:** It refers to loudness or softness. A firm and confident voice is a good starting point from which to make appropriate variations, for instance, by speaking more gently or more loudly.
- **Articulation:** It refers to the clarity of speech, which helps partners to understand the spoken words. When words come

out clearly and with proper gestures, then the understanding developed is much better.

- **Pitch:** It refers to the depth of one's voice. An optimum pitch range includes all the levels at which a pleasing voice can be produced without strain.
- **Emphasis:** A person may use emphasis when responding and when sharing feelings. A person using too much emphasis may seem melodramatic and one using too little emphasis may come across as wooden. Also, emphasis should not come at the wrong places.
- **Rate:** Speech rate is measured by words per minute. It depends not only on how quickly words are spoken, but also on the frequency and duration of pauses between them. If speaking too quickly, it indicates anxiety, and the partner may have difficulty in understanding them. On the other hand, a very slow rate of speech can appear boring. Therefore, pausing and being silent at the right times is another important aspect of speech rate.

Vocal Communication:

Vocal refers to spoken communication, specific to use of the voice. Voice is the most important thing in humans when it comes to being distinguished from other living beings. It is used as a major means of being able to convey our thoughts and feelings to the others.

Non-verbal communication

Behaviours that are effective non-verbal ways of conveying that the other is interested in and is open to listening includes smiling, leaning forward, making eye contact, gesturing and nodding one's head.

SOLER is composed of five important non-verbal skills.

S: face partner Squarely (that is, show interest and involvement in partner),

0: adopt Open posture, free from crossed arms and legs and showing non-defensiveness,

L: reminds one to Lean towards partner. Leaning too far and forward and being too close may be frightening but leaning too far away indicates disinterest.

E: represents Eye contact. Good eye contact with each other is a sign that one is attuned to partner, and

R: it is a reminder to Relax.

Some non-verbal communication skills are given below:

- Physical setting and seating arrangement
- Proximity preference
- Gestures and touch
- Facial expressions
- Eye contact
- Gaze
- Gestures
- Posture
- Appearance
- Body motion.

For example:

When there is something to be conveyed between partners, it is important that it is said in a correct setting of seating for both. The more comfortable the seating is and there is a harmonious surrounding, then the communication and ability to express feelings becomes easier and changes of developing understanding are better. Gestures and facial expressions reveal a lot about what the other person is thinking and thus interpretation of areas of concern can

be done. How partners make eye contact and gaze at each other tells a lot about how they feel about each other. It is always the eyes that give away the inner thoughts and feelings. Gestures and body motion also speak a great deal about a person. When someone is not ready for clear communication, he or she will express, by continuous body motion and gestures, discomfort when a topic of disinterest is started. In addition to these, how a person maintains his appearance at the time of conversations indicates his looking forward to or avoiding the talk.

When talking, gestures should complement our thoughts, motivations, and intentions. We should complement our words with our body language. By using eye contact, facial expressions, body movements and touch, we can better express our words and intentions. A partner's body language may make the other partner wonder: Does he listen actively? Does his body language match his words? Does he seem tense while listening? Is he impatiently awaiting the end of the communication?

A partner may receive the signal: My mind is closed, if one stands with his arms crossed. Continue speaking if you wish. There will be no acceptance. The body language speaks for itself if he is actively listening to the communication and eager to understand it. Our eyes are a mirror of our hearts. Maintain eye contact while communicating, avoiding eye contact is a strict no. The foundation of good relationships is transparent communication. This is a key to building trust. Whenever feelings are expressed honestly, tactics, diplomacy, and misunderstandings have no place.

Both partners enjoy clear and clean communication when they express themselves freely.

Communication is a skill of expressing our feelings and desires. It makes the receiver understand what is going on in the sender's mind, initiating feedback and thus understanding each other.

In fact, communication is a fundamental factor in a relationship; It is an important tool for a thriving relationship. We have been taught some basic etiquette in communication, like not to back-answer elders, saying 'Please', 'Thank you', and 'Sorry' at the right times. But using these phrases without feelings is pointless. There is a need to give proper training in good communication. But unfortunately, the need for imparting such training is not felt and no efforts are made in this direction.

It is an art to communicate. Respect should be shown to the other party involved. Inculcate, practice, and nurture this skill.

How can one communicate effectively?

Although everyone communicates differently, good communication has some basic characteristics in common. By practicing communication, you can learn, improve, and master it. Genuine communication is the key to effective communication.

The partner is not a mind reader 'Guess what's in my mind?' is a good fun game at the get-togethers. But it is not useful and can be dangerous at times. One's partner is neither a magician nor a mind reader. One may have an impression that my partner can correctly guess everything that goes on in my mind, but there are

chances that sometimes he may misconceive this. For e.g., silence when used to avoid hurting a partner when there is disagreement, may be misinterpreted as agreement. Now, one has two options. Either he allows the partner to guess, 'What is going on in my mind?' and later blame him for his wrong guess or honestly tell the partner what is in his mind.

It is true and has been proved by psychology that one himself is not completely aware of everything that is going on in his own mind. Then won't it be wrong to expect someone else to understand what is going on in one's mind? The earlier one realizes this fact, the easier it will be to achieve harmony in married life.

Communication styles - yours and mine

Everybody's method of communication is different. This does not make one method right and the other's wrong.

Some people are blunt in their expression. They speak their thoughts aloud. They do not hesitate to open up, even if they are aware that it may not be liked by the listener. Rather, they are not bothered about the impact of their expression on others. They do not speak goody-goody words in order to please others.

Some people anticipate others' reactions, before they express themselves. They care for the other's feelings.

Some people mumble. Without touching the point, they keep beating around the bush. These people themselves are not aware of what they want to say.

Communication skills of women and men are different.

If the mother tongue and/or the knowledge language, i.e., the language used as a medium of education, of the partners is different, they may face difficulty while communicating. They

should be aware of this fact and should make an additional effort to exchange effective communication.

There are many methods of communication. The possibility of their communication methods being different cannot be denied. So, both should understand and learn each other's method of communication.

Communication Techniques

Whatever we have to say, we should be able to say honestly without any inhibitions or reservations. It should be said clearly and without talking in a roundabout way. Our communication should clearly express our point of view and our intention behind it. Our response to the partner's statements/opinions/ arguments should also be clear. For, e.g., if you get hurt when your partner says something, make him understand it by saying, "It hurts. Please do not talk like this!" If you say this clearly, he will understand your feelings.

Tone: Often the tone and texture of speaking is more important than what is said. The rude, arrogant, angry tone of a speaker is very insulting for the listener. For e.g., try this statement in three different tones, in a persuasive tone, with anger and with love, "I cannot help you."

Stress on words: The stress given on some words supplements their meaning. Stress on different words in a sentence changes its meaning. For example, when you say, 'You know what I say,' try

to emphasize one word at a time and note the difference. Similarly, try one more sentence putting stress on these words one be one. 'Do **you** understand what I mean?' 'Do you **understand** what I mean?'

Communication with a touch of humour:

- Laughter is the best medicine.
- Smiling helps to resolve several issues.
- Smiling is an effective way to win over people.
- Laughter helps in defusing a stressful situation.
- Laughter secretes endorphins and other chemicals in the human body. Laughter has the power to change our bad mood and make us feel happy. Laughter helps us to overcome our pain and sorrow.
- Everyone loves a person with a smiling face. Such people play an important role in maintaining relationships.
- Laughing at one's own mistakes, cracking jokes on one's own stupidity are considered to be charactaristics of a mentally healthy personality.

One needs to make judicious use of humour, lest he steps on some one's feelings thereby causing more harm than good.

Good quality humour is difficult. Humour with sarcasm may create a frustrating experience. Sarcasm and humour are different. Sarcastic comments may make us laugh at times, but it is not humour. This should definitely be avoided.

Remarks ridiculing the partner and use of demeaning words must be avoided at all cost. Always laugh with others and NOT at others.

Active listening

In order to ensure uninterrupted flow of conversation among the partners, one has to listen actively when the other is talking.

Face each other while talking. To make conversation effective, avoid any other activity while communicating, for e.g. watching television, using a cell phone, reading a newspaper etc. Avoid conversation on unpleasant topics during meals. In essence, focus on communication.

There is a difference between hearing and listening. Active listening is way above only listening. Everyone has the ability to understand, show/express affection and trust. Communication which is backed by empathy goes beyond mere listening and facilitates understanding. This is called active listening.

Love language

Everyone's mental set-up is different, so everyone has a different way of thinking and behaving. Similarly each person expresses love in a different way. Everyone has his or her own language of love. Any partner will appreciate and feel very happy if his partner reflects his love language while communicating.

When the partners cheer up each other, a strong bond of trust is created. Small things like this may result in to a miraculous effect and develop trust. It gives pleasure and joy when one knows that his partner is taking care of his feelings. Instead of creating puzzles for each other and wasting time and energy in solving them, it is better to spend time in experiencing love in life.

That is why partners should understand each other's love language. Especially if the love language of both the partners is different, understanding it makes it easier to please each other.

Care to be Taken:

Under any circumstances, one should not insult or humiliate the person he or she is talking to. There are some important things to be avoided. They are as important as communication.

Things to avoid while communicating:

1. Arriving at conclusions hastily.
2. Being defensive when things are going against us.
3. Being aggressive.
4. Merely debating or arguing without finally arriving at a decision.
5. Behaving like enemies.
6. Being pessimistic.
7. Damaging the self-respect of the partner.
8. Discouraging the partner.
9. Falling prey to malicious practices of people instigating us against our partner.
10. Changing the subject during discussion, sidetracking the main issue.
11. Meaningless clutter.
12. Speaking impulsively without thought.

These are some humiliating remarks which insult the listener. Avoid them at all costs-

- If you really love me... (here we are doubting his love.)
- I cannot tolerate the way in which you behave… (we disrespect his behavior.)
- You love cricket, music etc., more than you love me.
- You're always... or you never... (it is criticizing.)
- You are just like your mother... (indirectly talking badly about his parents.)

- I do not think you will ever change....
- You have changed a lot....

Etiquette and Magical Words

There is a need to follow some etiquette while communicating. Use words like **'Thank you', 'I'm wrong', 'Sorry'** generously. But using these phrases without feelings is pointless because their genuineness or lack of it filters down to the listener immediately.

Apology: Apology and forgiveness are great characteristics of our personality. It is human to commit mistakes. Intentionally, or otherwise, our words and actions may hurt others. Words are like swords. They may badly hurt the receiver. Such words create obstacles in emotional relationships. "Time" is the only healer, but memories are not wiped out easily. An apology can heal all the bad effects.

If our partner is saying something, enough time should be given to him. We should not interrupt him in the middle of a conversation.

Once he has expressed himself, we should respond and put forth our opinion. Thus, he will know that we are listening to him. Body language could be effectively used for this purpose.

Letter Writing – An Effective Way of Communication

We can express our feelings effectively with the help of a letter. Writing a letter is an important tool for maintaining a relationship. If a partner is non-communicative, then writing letters is a useful way to interact.

Sometimes we want our partner to understand something but cannot tell him openly, directly, then writing a letter is a good option in such a situation.

Writing a letter serves two purposes:

We can express our feelings in a better way through a letter.

Negative emotions can be better expressed through a letter. Once expressed they lose their severity.

Communication can be more effective with the use of new technologies like Email, WhatsApp etc.

Incommunicative Partner

Some individuals do not express themselves freely. It is not bad per se, but they may be misunderstood and mistaken to be a snob. Suppose a husband is incommunicative, how can his wife make him talk? By helping him express his feelings, assuring him that she is interested in listening to him. To start with, she should talk about herself. Later, instead of bombarding him with questions, she should ask him a few selected questions which will motivate him to speak.

It should be accepted that he is not very communicative. Involve him in a dialogue. Respect his behavior and even appreciate him when he communicates. People are not born incommunicative, but this nature is developed due to some of their early experiences. The root cause can be pinpointed by observing and analyzing certain factors. 'Haste is waste,' hence one should not press one's partner to express himself.

For a partner who is less communicative

Normally a talkative partner must bear the responsibility for adjustments. But a less communicative partner should also put in equal efforts. One needs to assure his/her talkative partner that he/she is not avoiding communicating but it is his/her nature.

He should request his talkative partner to understand his difficulty and be patient. There is a need to examine the reason why one fears communicating with others. One may be skeptical that others will misuse his personal information. The root of a non-expressive nature may be some unpleasant childhood experience. One may be imitating his incommunicative parent.

Then one starts keeping his thoughts to himself when he is criticized heavily after having said something. Forgetting these experiences, he should share his life experiences from the past with his partner. Accepting his shyness openly he should try to overcome it.

Every day try to respond positively to what your spouse says to you by using phrases such as, "I'm so happy for you," "I was feeling bad to hear this," "I'm angry at what happened."

Modern Communication Methods

New methods of communication are developed in modern times. There are numerous options like Facebook, Email, and so on. The new generation likes texting more than a face-to-face or phone conversation. The boundaries of communication are expanding but depth is lacking. Sometimes speaking face to face is more effective than texting. Of course, sometimes such options are convenient and then they will take precedence.

When we communicate with our partner these heartfelt feelings are easily understood.

The genuineness of feelings is reflected through the eyes, and this infuses faith. Touch makes us blossom, and an embrace creates union. This love language binds both in an emotional bond. Thus, this love communication is a welcome experience which everyone always looks forward to experiencing, over and over again.

Section
4

Dissonant Music

1. Conflict Resolution

2. Imperfect Tunes

3. How to Handle Separation.

4. Infidelity

1

Conflict Resolution

"Peace is not absence of conflict; it is the ability to
handle conflict by peaceful means."

- Ronald Reagan

It is possible for two people to speak effectively through dialogue when they respect one another's opinions, understand and explain one another's positions and there is argument when one doesn't listen to the other's viewpoint completely and hastily decides that it's the wrong viewpoint, and then tries to convince the other that his/her standpoint is the only right one.

Arguments are often sparked by misunderstandings, biases, and opinions. Conflict can result from people making assumptions and not listening to the other person. Emotions can also fuel arguments, making people less likely to compromise and more likely to escalate the conflict.

Living together in conflict:

A conflict arises when neither of the partners are willing to listen to the other's views and they hastily and adamantly form

their own opinion that the other's viewpoint is wrong. In such a scenario, one or both try to persuade the other that your views are wrong and mine are correct.

It is not wrong to say that conflicts, quarrels, and differences of opinion are inevitable in a couple's peaceful co-existence.

But look at the following two statements:

'The more the quarrels, the more the abyss between a husband and wife and this is a major reason to worry.'

And

'The lesser the quarrels/conflicts, the more they love each other.'

Both the statements are neither 100% true nor false, but half-truths.

To understand this, four things must be considered-

1. Why do quarrels and differences of opinion exist?
2. What is the intensity and nature of it?
3. How much is the partner to blame?
4. How long does it take for a quarrel to be resolved?

There are differences, conflicts even at the beginning of a journey as a couple but they are not very intense or serious. They are often put aside and instead of taking it to the extreme, there is a strong possibility of a reconciliation as the relationship is in a romantic state. But once the initial phase is crossed and when it is time to consolidate the relationship, it is realized that both have very different psychological make-up.

Research has shown that when there is a discord between a couple, each one's body language and mental state affects the other. One word leads to another and voices are raised to the limit. Banging of doors, throwing things around occurs. Sometimes

there is actual physical assault as well. One partner expresses anger, rage, hatred, sorrow, pain etc. and as a result the other one answers back in the same token. It is a vicious cycle. Nobody knows how to put an end to it.

When are differences of opinion beneficial?

If we look at the differences of opinion from a positive point of view, we get the strength to look at life in a new perspective. When the differences are handled appropriately, the relationship becomes stronger. Both the partners can learn something from it. One can use this as an opportunity to identify one's shortcomings. One gets a chance to understand that, though different, the partner's viewpoint may be better than mine.

If the difference of opinion is handled as a win-win situation, it can provide a good solution. This relationship can certainly go a step ahead.

Effects of conflicts

Conflict between couples has far-reaching effects. It can cause a decrease in self-esteem, increased anxiety, stress, emotional breakdown, social effects, and even depression. It can even cause physical health problems in many cases. Conflicts can be traumatic and have all the effects associated with traumatic situations. (Please refer to 'Before You Find a Counsellor' by Dr Pratibha Deshpande).

Let us understand the effect of conflict on the human brain

The human brain can respond to conflict in a variety of ways, involving several different brain systems and regions. Individual differences in coping strategies, emotional regulation, and resilience can be explained by understanding the neural mechanisms underlying conflict responses. Additionally, it provides insights into how interventions, that target specific brain

systems or pathways, may mitigate the adverse effects of conflict on mental health. Here are some of the key effects of conflict on the brain:

1. **Amygdala Activation:** Conflict tends to activate the amygdala, a brain region involved in processing emotions, particularly fear and aggression. Conflict is associated with emotional arousal, including anger, anxiety, and distress.

2. **Prefrontal Cortex Involvement:** It is important to note that the prefrontal cortex, especially the dorsolateral prefrontal cortex (DLPFC) and the anterior cingulate cortex (ACC), play a crucial role in cognitive control and decision making during conflict. In response to conflict stimuli, these regions help regulate emotional responses, evaluate options, and plan action.

3. **Sympathetic Nervous System Activation:** (Stress mechanism) Conflict often activates the sympathetic nervous system, triggering the body's "fight or flight" response. This physiological arousal is associated with increased heart rate, blood pressure, and stress hormone release (such as cortisol and adrenaline), preparing the body to respond to perceived threats.

4. **Hypothalamic-Pituitary-Adrenal (HPA) Axis Activation:** The HPA axis, a complex neuroendocrine system involving the hypothalamus, pituitary gland, and adrenal glands, is activated during conflict. This leads to the release of cortisol, a stress hormone that helps mobilize energy resources and modulate the body's response to stress factors.

5. **Reward and Punishment Systems:** The ventral striatum and the orbitofrontal cortex are brain regions involved in reward

and punishment processing. Conflict-related decisions are evaluated in these regions by weighing both benefits and risks.

6. **Interplay of Neurotransmitters**: Dopamine, serotonin, and noradrenaline are neurotransmitters that modulate mood, motivation, and arousal during conflict. Emotional reactivity, impulse control, and stress resilience can be affected by dysregulation of these neurotransmitter systems.

7. **Neural Plasticity**: Chronic or severe conflict experiences can lead to structural and functional changes in the brain, including alterations in synaptic connectivity, neurochemical balance, and neural circuitry. These changes may contribute to long-term effects on behavior, cognition, and mental health.

It is clear from all these effects that conflict is undesirable and detrimental to the system and that avoiding or resolving it as soon as possible is always the best course of action.

From Differences of Opinion to Conflict:

It is not wrong to have differences, the method of handling them could be wrong. The following are the steps to handle conflict:

Step1: *Differences and their discussion, debates:* Differences exist in every two individuals. It involves shifting our perspective and understanding the other person's viewpoint. In this, both partners explain their role, opinion, reason, and try to understand each other.

Step2: *In Presumptions*: both partners understand each other's opinions, and consider feasible outcomes from both perspectives, aiming for a reasonable win/win situation. They weigh what is right and suitable for both parties rather than focusing solely on one's own perspective, deciding whose opinion to accept or making decisions based on whose opinion is determined. Generally, this

decision is made based on whose argument seems more acceptable. That means if there's a disagreement within a couple about whether the wife should work or not, the final decision should be hers, and if this decision is made in favour of the other partner, then they should accept it. This is the path of mutual victory. If a decision is made based on one's opinion, the other partner shouldn't say, "You didn't consider my opinion," nor should it be taken as an insult. Because ultimately, they are the person the other loves. True, isn't it?

Step 3: *Heated Arguments:* This is the next step after argumentation and debate. It involves belittling the other person's opinions and ridiculing the other person's thoughts without maintaining emotional balance, making one's own viewpoint dominant, often leading to verbal attacks. They bring up past grievances, trying to score points against each other's families, and seek to humiliate the other. During such times, past disagreements resurface, causing bitterness. Memories of sacrifices made for each other are thrown back in each other's faces, tallying up who did what for whom. Gradually, the balance between both partners is lost. They attempt to outshout each other, voices keep rising, with no one willing to yield. At such moments, a productive resolution becomes impossible, and instead of solid or beneficial compromises, it's more likely to end up in a stalemate. This situation can be likened to a ticking time bomb of danger because our rational thinking is clouded by emotions. Both partners are unable to understand each other's perspectives amidst the chaos. The possibility of resolving conflicts diminishes as time goes on. Moreover, the potential for further arguments and deteriorating circumstances increases. Listening to each other may seem insulting at times. Mental anguish ensues, damaging one's self-

esteem. If there isn't deep love, profound friendship, or emotional maturity, then arguments escalate further.

Step 4: *Battle:* Blaming each other, pulling out past mistakes, trying to dominate, refusing to listen to each other's side, harbouring resentment over personal issues - all these signs of discord are still prevalent. One starts seeing the other not as a beloved but as an enemy. The other's actions constantly remind one of the troubles they faced because of them. The phrase, "Love for you is a big mistake in this lifetime," is used to mock the partner. At such times, the other partner also doesn't hold back from engaging in harmful behaviour. He becomes the enemy in every sense to the other partner. It's as if the rivalry between the two has been carried over from past lives. All their weapons are out against each other, metaphorically speaking. Sometimes, it turns into physical violence, shouting matches, and brawls, leaving both bruised emotionally. This continues for many days or even years until they finally reconcile. Many couples remain stuck in this cycle, firmly entrenched in their positions. The years pass by, but the turmoil within their homes doesn't cease. Children bear witness to these fights, and it becomes natural for them. As they grow older, they become accustomed to the conflict.

Although emotional intelligence is crucial, it's not given much importance. Couples often advise each other to be more emotionally mature, but seldom do they have the time or inclination to work on themselves. Easy living dulls their senses, and even if they realize it early on, they don't seek guidance or counselling. Men, in particular, tend to protect their egos, avoid seeking help and are resistant to change. Women are more inclined to seek guidance and also work on themselves. This is my experience. However,

relationships can still improve with concerted efforts from both parties. Otherwise, it's the end of the road for the relationship.

Step 5: *Enmity/ Animosity:* This is when the feeling of a relationship is permanently over. The idea of separating becomes a real possibility. Besides parting ways, there seems to be no other option. And such a divided group doesn't even consider reconciliation as an option. Year after year, they'll be entangled in legal battles, as neither wants to give in to the other. They don't easily want to give the other person a chance or ease the situation for them. They want to teach them a lesson. They don't realize that their money is being spent on lawyers like water. The youthful years of their lives go waste. It's a tragedy of simple living. Here, simple living comes to an end. Ultimately, it's the fourth leg of the relationship that's over.

In the viewpoint of the counsellor:

Until the first two stages, disagreements can be beneficial. Both partners have a common goal until this point: to resolve issues through discussion and find a solution that benefits both parties, providing a useful tool for their lives, leading them towards the right path. However, negative emotions start to build up in the final three stages.

If both partners exhibit arrogance, pride, negativity, stubbornness, and self-centred behaviour, the disagreement escalates beyond the second stage, reaching the final three stages. In this stage differences turns into conflicts Merely resolving disagreements through compromise and making informed decisions becomes impossible. The focus shifts to proving oneself right, asserting dominance, and blaming the partner. This blame

game and emotional manipulation become the primary focus, severely damaging the chances of happiness.

In the beginning, they tend to adopt a confrontational stance, escalating minor disagreements into intense conflicts. Consequently, they fail to control their emotions, which leads to an increase in the intensity of their arguments. While handling disagreements, it's essential to consider what your ultimate goal is. Is asserting "I am right, it's my way or the highway," essential for your happiness and joy? The mindset of argumentativeness and "it's my way or the highway" attitude doesn't contribute positively to resolving conflicts. In matters of love, compromise is essential. Winning isn't the most important aspect.

In conflict the objective is to prove how the partner is wrong. Then the main aim becomes blaming, hurting and exploiting the partner. These are the most damaging points for a happy married life. As differences accumulate, they assume a huge and fierce proportion from the time they are initially quite small. Their intensity can be reduced if they are given proper channels to vent from time to time. In order to handle differences, one must think about what one really wants.

Is this what we want? To prove how right we are rather than seeking happiness and joy?

Mere reasoning and the attitude 'I am right,' is not useful for resolving a conflict amicably.

There must be understanding if relationships of love are to be preserved. Winning is not at all important in such relationships.

Types of conflict:

The three main kinds of conflicts are:

1   Conflicts over solvable differences.
2.   Conflicts over gridlocked problems.
3.   Conflict over perpetual problems.

1. Conflicts over solvable problems

Solvable problems can be solved easily with certain measures and proper communication. It may or may not require an expert's advice.

Characteristics:

1.   Lack of communication can be solved by educating couples about the importance of communication.
2.   Inability to understand the partner's desires and ambitions leads to conflicts. There are differences in the nature and personalities of both parties. For example, one is talkative and the other reticent, one spends money thoughtfully and the other lavishly.
3.   A difference that can be remedied is the loss of trust and loyalty caused by infidelity and the conflicts that result. It could be remedied by a heartfelt apology, forgiveness, and compensation.
4.   Regular but intense differences that are not connected with major problems: differences caused by a lack of emotional intelligence, which are not handled and resolved in a timely manner. As an example, one of the two is very neat and clean, while the other is careless.
5.   Making a mountain out of a molehill.
6.   Some partners can end the differences only via conflict and quarrel.
7.   Differences about financial dealings/transactions.

8. In the case of problems in the bedroom, there is a possibility that an expert's advice is needed.

9. Adjustment with family members like the parents-in-law, brothers, and sisters-in-law etc.

10. Repeated quarrels on the same point: If a couple is quarrelling frequently over the same issue, it means that there is a deep-rooted problem. In such situations, it is necessary to stop quarrelling and identify the problem. Once the problem is identified, it becomes easy to find a solution for it. That is why both should agree on finding out the basic problem first.

11. Conflicts arising out of misunderstandings.

2. Conflicts over gridlocked problems

Gridlock problems occur when couples are unable to communicate openly, honestly, and effectively with each other. A lack of trust, misunderstandings, or a lack of respect for each other's opinions can lead to these issues. They are a little difficult to solve and may require an expert's advice.

Characteristics:

1. Both the partners are adamant on their points. Nobody is ready to listen to the other's point of view, so they keep on repeating the same thing.

2. Nobody is ready to accept a submissive attitude. No effort is made to find a way out of the problem.

3. This kind of disagreement creates a mental tension between both. Each one feels that my partner is not listening to me and respecting me.

4. The problems or disagreements that initially appeared small, trivial, or even funny become severe and trouble them on the

emotional level. Emotional differences between them reach an extreme point and a drift away from each other sets in.

5. There could be a lot of causes for gridlocked problems. For example, should we have a child now or should we wait for some more time, should we be open fisted now or should we save for old age, etc.

3. Conflict over perpetual problems

Conflicts between couples that never seem to be resolved are perpetual conflicts. Conflicts can range from minor issues such as disagreement on how to raise children to larger issues such as differences in religious beliefs or money management. In relationships, perpetual conflicts can lead to mistrust and resentment. Such conflicts require an expert's advice.

Characteristics:

1. If there are a lot of dissimilarities in their personalities and lifestyle, some differences keep on occurring again and again. This is possible in everyone's case, the nature of the differences change.

2. Some differences can be quite easy for one couple to resolve while some other couple might find the same differences tough and complicated.

3. Differences of opinion could be of any type. A few couples constantly quarrel over the same cause, but it does not harm their coexistence. Both know how much importance is to be given to those quarrels. They have accepted their differences as a part of their life. For some couples such differences are a matter of life and death and these differences affect their relationship deeply.

4. These conflicts are like a tangle that cannot be unravelled. In every round of discussions on the differences, each one hurts the other more and more. Mudslinging occurs.

As a result, both get irritated, depressed, pained, and hurt. Their conscience is lost. The best way out is to accept the differences and go ahead. It can be the case that there are differences and there is no agreement. It is not necessary that two separate individuals agree with each other every time. Once the differences are accepted, there are no fierce arguments and no emotional slashings and therefore there is no irritation or hurt. From this standpoint, mutual trust and love is maintained.

Body language and conflict:

Body language plays a great role in conflict. When a couple gets into conflict, their body language is different, which hurts both. Voices are raised and become shrill. Anger or helplessness is expressed through the eyes.

- The body becomes stiff and starts sweating; the pulse and heartbeats increase.
- A concrete or beneficial way out of the quarrel cannot be reached at this stage. This physical state is a warning bell because in this state one loses his/her ability to deliberate. None is in a state to understand the other's mental condition. The possibility of resolving the quarrel amicably is lost.
- Arguments beyond this stage could lead to more deterioration of the situation. One's body language, way of speaking, tone of speech, looks etc. can add to the deterioration.
- The listener may find it insulting.
- In this state they are mentally disturbed, there is low self-esteem, and the self-image is damaged. This can lead to

physical conditions like cough and cold, psychosomatic diseases can occur, blood pressure may rise and there is even a possibility of a heart attack.

It is extremely important to end the arguments as soon as possible. One can choose any one of the following options by mutual approval.

Three ways of resolving differences of opinion

The ways to handle differences of opinion are:

1. **To reach a golden mean/meeting in the middle:** It is expected to find a mid-way solution. For example, he wants to have tea in the morning whereas she drinks coffee. The golden mean could be that he makes tea for both on one day and the next day she makes coffee for both.

2. **Meeting on your side:** Discussing the differences and then accepting any one's opinion with positivity. The one whose opinion is not accepted, will have to forego his/her stand. Here comes a sacrifice. For example, the husband does not want to have a child but understanding the wife's feelings and love, he agrees later to have a child.

3. **Meeting Later:** Postponing the discussion on the differences. Instead of accepting anyone's opinion, the decision is kept pending. If the discussion is not resulting in a conclusive one, it is better to postpone it for a while. The postponement could be for a few days, months or even for a few years. During this period there should be no bitterness between the two due to the differences, they should help each other lovingly. Both should decide that this difference should not be a hindrance to their marital happiness. If there is no agreement on a certain point, this is the best option. As time passes those points may

become less significant or possibilities of more solutions may also come up. A partner's opinion may also change. Lifetime postponement is also possible and then time will present a solution to you.

Some solutions may not be 'right' or 'wrong'. For example, whether a movie should have a happy or tragic end. Each one's liking could be different. The husband may like comedy and the wife may like family-oriented movies or tragedies. In such cases both are right.

4. **Friendly settlement and not compromise:** Both should listen to each other's viewpoints and understand the feelings behind it. Many times, it happens that what our partner wants is something entirely different. Accepting the partner's view or opinion is not going to bring us any loss. Or, even if there is some loss, it could be insignificant. In such situations we must consider the partner's intentions. His/her intention could be emotional, beyond logic or reason. If this is accepted openly, it will be a win-win situation.

Skills required for of resolving conflicts

Generally, to end any differences, logic, rational and critical thinking, persuasion skills, emotional and social competence, active listening, awareness about the natural differences between a man and a woman, awareness about each-other's emotions, the method of handling the conflict are all very useful. There are many other factors which we have discussed in each chapter.

A conflict should not be viewed as a tragedy but as an opportunity. A diamond shines only when properly cut. Similarly, a personality does not flower without multiple aspects, and this must

be done consciously. Emotions are stronger than logic. Even then, without giving in to them, one must handle a conflict at times.

Precautions to be taken while handling differences

Arguments, conflicts, quarrels don't get any solutions unless they are handled skillfully. Or otherwise, they only create distances and dissatisfactions. We have seen that differences can be resolved without heated arguments; but the main challenge is not to go beyond the first three steps.

We want a good solution that will be applicable to both the partners.

What do we want, happiness or to prove that I am right? What will we gain if we are proven to be right, sulking or fondling our ego? A little give and take, accepting the other's view at times with pleasure, a little mockery and pulling his/her leg, a serious quarrel or to displease and hurt the partner by proving that I am right? We want to have happiness and pleasure in life; we do not want marital life to be a battlefield.

Bad memories to be erased as soon as possible

Some negative incidents remain in our memory, and they are never wiped out. Partners living a happy life don't give much importance to such negativities but consciously enhance the positive aspects. But, if life together is not a happy one, our memory reminds us of the negative things adding spice to it and making bad events excessively large.

For Example:

Madhuri and Ramesh are heading towards a divorce after fifteen years of married life. They want to save the marriage for their son, and they are seeking the help of a counselor.

"In the past fifteen years only one good thing happened to me and that is my son. Rest everything is bad," Madhuri said. *"I didn't have a single happy day in the past fifteen years,"* Ramesh added.

From the perspective of a counsellor:

- Though they talk of saving the marriage their behavior doesn't reflect their thoughts. The presence of imperfect tunes has made their life hopeless.

- After proper counselling, the couple found a new way to live together happily.

Successful efforts of compromise/ reconciliation

During a quarrel, under an emotional surge, we hurt our partner. Now is the time to ask for forgiveness. In a quarrelsome mood, both the minds have got scratches on them, they need to be healed. Everyone's method of asking for forgiveness could be different but both should most certainly say to each other,

"Sorry, I hurt you. Please forgive me."

Thereafter, both should compromise and reconcile.

For example, going together somewhere for dinner/lunch, making and drinking coffee together, giving sweet smiles, kissing, hugging, etc.

Remember conflict is not the 'end of relationship'

Physical and psychological aloofness distances the couple from each other even more. If they get timely and proper help, both can come together again. Of course, both should be ready to take help.

When should a counsellor be contacted?

In the following situation, a counsellor's visit helps to resolve the conflict.

- When the arguments are extreme and neither partner or only one partner is willing to reconcile.
- While finding solutions, both are on different paths with the attitude of 'you and yours' and 'me and mine'.
- Both are living a parallel life, both tend to be lonely.
- Sometimes both or one of them prefer remaining outside the house, indulging in drinking or infidelity as a way out.
- When one partner or both partners feel that a divorce is inevitable. At such moments, please keep in mind that the relationship is not completely over. There is a ray of hope. There will be no need to end the marriage. The only thing is that both have to make conscious efforts for that. A counsellor needs to be contacted.

Positivity is the insurance in married life. It guarantees repeated efforts of repairing the spoiled relationship and reduces the tension. At any stage of togetherness, it refreshes the relationship between the partners. It renews the friendship between the two.

2

Imperfect Tunes

"Being happy doesn't mean, that everything is perfect. It means that you've decided to look beyond the imperfections," Gerard Way.

We can see the following as our enemies when we talk about relationships:

1. Misunderstanding.
2. Criticism
3. Contempt
4. Defensiveness
5. Stonewalling
6. Stubbornness
7. Fault finding
8. External locus of control
9. Distrust, suspicious nature

Let us see each of these factors

1. Misunderstandings

Misunderstanding refers to misinterpreting an event, act, or behavior and believing the misinterpretation to be true. Misunderstanding occurs when we fail to understand correctly. An improper observation and evaluation of a disagreement, a difference of opinion, one's words and/or behavior is a

misunderstanding. When you misinterpret your partner's words and act based on someone else's words, misunderstanding occurs.

2. Criticism

Criticism can be viewed as a means of exhibiting or expressing dislike. When we disagree with someone's choice, we criticize them. Direct criticism is preceded by denial, disapproval, dislike, resistance, opposition, objection, complaint, slander, insult, and contempt. It is caused by differences in likes and dislikes, in personalities, and in thinking.

We criticize everyone and everything, including movies, plays, and books we read, but none of that matters to the person involved. The criticism we give a near one does make a difference to him/her. It depends on the nature of the criticism and the listener's mentality whether the change is for the better or worse.

Whenever we criticize, we raise an objection, point out a difference, or try to draw attention to our own viewpoint. We put the relationship at stake by proving 'how I am good, and the other is bad' without even realizing it. Two words sharpen criticism: 'always' and 'never'. It may become a habit to attack the other person's mentality unknowingly. Constant criticism can damage self-confidence and self-respect. Relationships are less accepted due to a decline in mentality. The process of bringing such a person out of their cocoon is difficult after they have become trapped in it. **For clarity, let's take an example:**

What will be Maya's reaction when her partner Rajiv returns home late every day?
Complaint:
Maya will say, "Why are you always late?"

In the beginning, the complaint is like this, with a note of affection and care in it. However, the reason may be trivial. Complaints are often caused by differences in likes and dislikes. Their gravity increases if they are not addressed properly.

Objection:

Initially, the criticism is mild, but gradually becomes more forceful. Suddenly, everything seems objectionable.

Maya will say, "It has become quite routine now. Why do you stay in the office so late?"

Anger:

The voice is now vehement, heated, and filled with anger.

'I can't stand you coming home so late every day! Aren't you concerned about us?'

The act of contempt:

"You've become so self-centered that you can't see beyond yourself. Can't you come home on time?" The nature of the partner is targeted here.

Control:

"I won't take your late return, I don't want it. It's important for you to be on time and follow the rules. You must listen to me."

In this case, the mentality of a dictator who decides everything is quite evident. There is no awareness that the other person might have a different opinion. It is expected that the partner should listen without questioning back.

Worry/anxiety:

It has two expressions.

"Oh, Rajiv, why so late? You don't even bother to call me up. I get worried but you have no concern for that."

Even though the words come out of worry about Rajiv, the method is one of blaming him.

"Oh, Rajiv, why are you so late? It worries me. I urge you not to do this. If you plan to arrive late, please call me before you leave. My heart aches for you." Here Maya is urging since she genuinely gets worried.

Sarcastic criticism:

In this, an incident is related to the total personality of the partner because the speaker goes on talking without thinking. Many times, this is something unjust and troublesome. The tone is of blame, so the next conversation turns into a heated debate. If the tone of criticism persists, a distance is created between the two; both the personalities get affected which can result in disagreement and antagonism. The one who is criticized feels insulted. The self-image is hurt, and the person starts to debate to prove that he/she is not what is being projected by the criticism. Then the partner also goes into debate and starts criticizing. 'Always' and 'never' sharpen the criticism. The main point is lost and the whole debate goes on a totally different track.

3. Contempt

How do we define contempt or insult?

Insults are expressions of scorn or derision. The feeling of contempt manifests itself in disrespect or disregard for someone or something. Contempt and insults can be verbal or nonverbal.

- Intimidation occurs when there is a feeling that 'I am better than you'. A mixture of anger and hatred also contributes to it. Contempt is an expression of disrespect and is intensified by insulting words.

- Contempt is born of sarcastic words and derision. The result of extreme anger and hatred is constant contempt and insult. Divorce can result from this.

- The insulter may start to view the partner as an emotionless, lifeless object because of the insult. A partner may counter charge, mudsling, go away or stand still in self-defense in such a situation. This cannot lead to a win-win situation. There is a possibility that if it is done repetitively, it will result in a divorce.

- As soon as these differences are reached the point of blaming their parents, the debate spirals out of control. The blame is placed on family lineages. Personal insults can be tolerated, but insults directed at one's parents or family cannot.

  As an example, when the partner says,

  "I have noticed that you intentionally bother me."

  "This is not surprising; can I expect anything else from you?"

  "It is very clear, in the end, you will behave like your parents."

  Warning in this case: things can reach a point of no return or the extreme point of divorce.

4. Defensiveness

The act of being defensive involves feeling threatened and responding with an argumentative or hostile attitude. The act can be seen as a way to protect oneself from criticism or blame. Insecurity and fragility are often indicators of defensiveness.

If we think that our partner will attack us verbally, mentally, or physically, we start complaining beforehand, pretending to be an innocent victim, and such behavior indicates defensiveness.

It is conveyed to the partner that "actually, you are wrong, I am not".

As an example, "How am I supposed to clean the kitchen platform after cooking? Cooking plus cleaning? Am I supposed to do both? Sorry not possible. It's a pain!"

This adds to the conflict because it is a matter of the partner's expectations.

There point that is made is that it is incorrect of the partner to expect and to voice expectations.

If we go on the defensive based only on a suggestion or a few words from our partner, it is likely it will disturb the harmony. The best way out is to listen to the partner's complaints and acknowledge that we are also responsible for the problem.

5. Stonewalling

In order to ignore the partner's words completely, one creates a kind of impenetrable shield around themselves. Alternatively, one may simply leave without talking.

When one goes away, it can be escapism or contempt for one's Partner; stonewalling means one is physically present but mentally miles away.

The face may seem careless, or he/she may seem to be trying to calm down. There may be no emotions on the face, or it may appear as if it were a blank slate. This is an area where men lead. Therefore, women feel that the problem is very serious, but her partner is not interested in discussing it. It is a vicious circle when one feels like talking and the other doesn't. The moment we realize our partner is stonewalling, we need to press the pause button; this will save both of us. After a while, we'll be able to make our point more sensibly.

6.   Stubbornness

A stubborn partner can lead to disagreements, arguments, and resentment in a relationship. A stubborn spouse may refuse to compromise, consider the other's perspective, or take responsibility for their actions, resulting in tension and communication breakdowns. Additionally, it can result in feelings of frustration and hurt for the other partner, resulting in a lack of trust and intimacy. Long-term damage can occur if one partner is consistently stubborn and unwilling to change. To maintain a healthy and strong relationship, both partners must be willing to listen, understand, and work together.

7.   Fault finder

The fault finder is always looking for fault in everything. Even if everything is good, they are going to find some flaw in the other and find something to complain about. Stress and anxiety can result from this negative trait. Recognizing and acknowledging mistakes without being too harsh is important. The best way to deal with mistakes is to take responsibility for them and then learn from them. By doing so, people can grow and improve without feeling bad about themselves. Furthermore, being a fault finder can undermine trust and cooperation within a team. Rather than dwelling on what went wrong, it is important to find solutions to issues. The confidence individuals need to stay motivated and work together effectively can be gained by recognizing mistakes, taking responsibility for them, and striving to do better.

When one partner is a fault finder, they do destructive criticism, and the other partner will have a hard time and this can lead to feelings of resentment and low self-esteem.

8. External locus of control

The locus of control refers to the degree to which individuals believe they can influence the events and outcomes in their lives. A person's perception of how much they can influence their own actions and the outcome of those actions is described by this psychological concept. Individuals with an internal locus of control are more likely to take responsibility for their actions and believe their efforts will lead to desired outcomes. In order to achieve their goals, they may make proactive decisions, set goals, and take the necessary actions. Individuals with an external locus of control, however, may feel that their actions have little impact on the outcome and may rely more on luck or external circumstances. In case of failure, a person with internal locus of control will blame himself, while a person with external locus of control will blame others.

The partner with an external locus of control always blames the other partner for any mistake that happens. Having an external source of control has a negative impact on the other partner.

1. **Communication:** People with an external locus of control tend to blame outside factors for their problems or failures, which can lead to a lack of personal responsibility. They can create a barrier to effective communication and the Partner may become frustrated or feel unheard.

2. **Responsibility:** A partner with an internal locus of control may feel resentful or frustrated if they constantly feel responsible for the relationship. So, the partnership may feel imbalanced or unfair.

3. **Trust:** When one partner consistently blames external factors or the other partner for their problems, the other partner may lose confidence in their ability to handle challenges or take

responsibility. Trust can be eroded and the bond between partners can be strained as a result.

4. **Unresolved conflicts:** A partner with an external locus of control may avoid confronting difficult issues or problems, resulting in unresolved conflicts creating tension and resentment between partners. This can prevent healthy communication and problem-solving.

A locus of control that is external to the relationship can negatively impact communication, trust, and conflict resolution. To address and navigate these issues, both partners need to work together.

9.   Distrust and Suspicious Nature

It is possible for a one partner to lack trust if he/she has a suspicious nature. There can be arguments, accusations, and ultimately, damage to the marriage. It is injustice to another partner. Both partners may experience stress and anxiety, further straining their relationship.

Case study:

One day a sixty-year-old woman came for counseling in a delirious state.

After coming, she sat staring at a photo frame for some time.

I patted her on the shoulder without speaking, gave her water to drink,

After calming down, she began to speak,

"I have been married for forty-two years. But today I feel what have I gained by getting married? I have two wonderful children living abroad. I have four grandchildren,

and a loving husband. But yesterday I had doubts, does he really love me? I keep his house well, cook beautifully, treat all his relatives with hospitality, so he treats me with love. Does he really love me from the heart? I fell in love with him on my wedding day. He was busy with business, then it was my job to bring up the children, take care of their education and I put my soul to the test while doing it. I lived with just one thought, this is my family, and it is my duty to look after them well. Until yesterday this was my precious thought but day…but today, I think differently.

"It has been twenty years since my children moved to London. Now I am used to not having them. But at that time, I was overwhelmed. Only forty years old! I didn't know what to do with the rest of my life. Because so far, I only lived for them.

"The children were gone and six months later I had a crisis that I had never imagined," she said.

She paused for a moment,

"Shall I drink some water?'

"Sure, I'll make some coffee. Let's both of us have a cup of coffee."

When I brought coffee, she was crying hiding her face in her palms.

"Listen to me, let's have a coffee and then talk," I said.

She shook her head.

But without taking the coffee she started talking.

"My son's childhood friend came to visit us after the children left. I began to look for my children in him. My

days started to go well. Later I came to know that my son had sent him to us. To make up for my lack of children.

"As these days passed, one day, my husband insisted on my proving my fidelity." She stopped talking.

I got a thorn in my side. I got some idea of what happened.

"So...?" I asked.

"To my husband I was a woman, and he was a man. He forgot that I am a hurt mother and the man is young enough to be my son. Neither of us had gone out of the house even once. My husband forgot that in his presence we used to sit in the living room and just chat. My loving husband at that moment was just a skeptical husband."

Now her tears dried up.

I just kept patting her.

"Later...?"

"I convinced him. Took an oath of my children. I don't know if he understood, but he forgot temporarily. In two days, that boy also went to London to study. I forgot it as a bad dream. Some days or maybe years it was tough for me. Did he think of me only as a wife in the last twenty years? I did not get any answer to this question. But I did not forget that wound, but my mind understood. The last twenty years passed happily. But yesterday's incident made me think again, 'Why didn't I get a divorce twenty years ago? Why did I stay with someone who smeared my character?'"

"What happened yesterday?"

"Yesterday morning when we woke up and were drinking tea together, he said, 'How strange you were then.'

At first, I did not understand. But slowly it slipped into my mind, what he was talking about.

"'You thought I had forgotten, but for the past twenty years this incident has been in my memory.' He spoke poisonous words.

"Doctor, I want a divorce. I'll get one, won't I?"

From the counselor's point of view:

- For the first time in my life as a counsellor, I had no answer. It was entirely her decision.

- I suggested she should take two sessions and then take a decision.

- She did not take a divorce. Her husband came for counselling, apologized to her in a proper manner.

- Both are trying to take their marriage from ordinary to extraordinary.

These imperfect tunes spoil our relationships, it is a breakdown of trust and communication. And there are more chances of breakups, divorces. By recognizing the signs, we can address these emotions in ourselves, and in our partner, before they cause too much damage. If necessary, seek professional help.

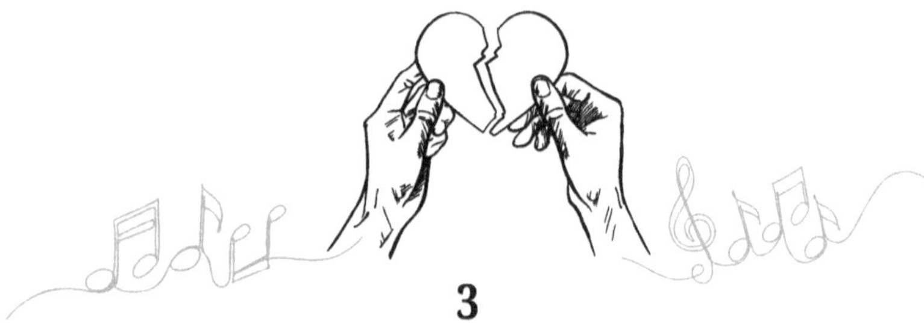

3

How to Handle Separation

"Both thought that as soon as they decide to stay together, only love will prevail, and life will be a bed of roses. And they realize, as time passes, that their lives are quite different from the ones they had imagined. One feels that my partner has changed a lot. He/she was a different person before."

Then the key question springs up- where has love disappeared?

The two of them had spent hours together looking into each other's eyes; now the same eyes are filled with anger, leaving them both depressed.

When he sees that the person who once called him 'my prince' is now fuming with rage, he is deeply troubled.

They were ready to die together earlier; now they swear they will never look at each other again. In the past, this person was an important part of my life. Why do I dislike him/her so much now?

It's a strange relationship, isn't it? A few days ago, the same eyes were filled with love, and now they are filled with hatred!

And either one of them or both want to separate. It is not the only option if you cannot get along with each other. The decision to separate is a tough decision and a weak one.

Why do relationships fail?

Despite being in love, romantic relationships and live-in relationships break up for a variety of reasons. Marriages break up despite being 'love marriages'. Why do divorces occur in arranged marriages, despite having chosen one of many and after gathering information about him/her before getting married?

A psychologist says, "Every marriage has the potential to be successful, but…."

This 'but' is very huge and full of meaning.

Of course, in some cases, this option is necessary. Though marriage is sacred, it is not a line on a stone that can't be wiped out. But really, is this decision always taken after a lot of thought? May be yes may be no.

Garry Chapman, a marriage counselor, says, "Separation occurs because of a lack of proper preparation for being together and not understanding and developing proper skills."

In 1994, based on scientific observations, Dr. John Gottman and his colleagues from the University of Washington declared, "If we carefully observe a couple only for fifteen minutes, we can recognize whether the marriage is going to stay or not; and 90% of the times our predictions come true." Is this true? We don't know. But it is true that a separation is a very unpleasant, hurtful, and painful experience.

When and how do things start going wrong?

Separation isn't something that happens overnight. It's not as if everything was fine until yesterday, there were no problems,

and then suddenly the only option is separation. Over time, the relationship becomes strained. It is evident that the distance between the two is growing. Our response is either to ignore this or to apply a temporary, superficial remedy. It becomes impossible to tolerate or adjust, so separation is sought.

Symptoms of a strained relationship:

- The partners become sad frequently. Instead of getting involved with each other they grow apart. There are frequent quarrels, tensions, irritation accompanied with short-tempered behaviour.
- Both the partners constantly insult and look down upon each other. They talk rudely to each other, ridicule and deride each other beyond limits.
- Either both or one of them fears expressing oneself, which is why there is no effective communication between them. A feeling of insecurity arises. As a result, they start avoiding each other which results in loneliness. This is a vicious circle.
- There is dishonesty or breach of trust and loss of trust in the partner.
- There is a lack of joint planning. Important aspects of the partner, his/her problems and likes and dislikes are neglected.
- Escapes like work, sport, addiction, social media, television, shopping etc. are sought to keep away from the partner.
- Only one's own good is constantly thought of in the co-existence.
- Physical relation is avoided or denied.
- There is no belief in love and there is a lack of energy, modesty, and respect for the partner.

- Both feel that there is nothing left to talk to each other. Rather, both don't feel like talking at all.
- The distance between the two increases and a rift is created.
- There is a need for help from experts.

Can separation be avoided in such cases?

It can be avoided, no doubt about it; but only if both decide they want this togetherness to last and make efforts accordingly. To maintain a relationship, full-hearted and positive efforts must be made. Positive thoughts will lead to positive behavior, and they will preserve the relationship when they walk in that direction. I think it's worth trying as there is no guarantee that the next relationship will last. Relationships in the future are much tougher since memories of previous relationships will have adverse effects.

Factors of separation:

Factors in each case could be different. Many times, the fundamental cause is different from the apparent cause; and many times, both the partners are not even aware of the fundamental cause. In previous chapters, we have already discussed in detail how to stay happily together. We have warned also that failing to do so will have adverse effects on relationships. Now we know the reasons why some couples were unable to remain together. The list could be quite long.

Of course, some causes need to be considered seriously. They are:

- When the partner has a violent nature and resorts to mental and physical abuse
- Infidelity, extramarital relations.

- Partner engages in some addiction.
- Partner who has a serious, incurable physical disease
- Partner who has AIDS
- Partner having psychological illness or mental disorders.

The list could go on and on. Whether to go in for a separation for these reasons depends on the intensity of the reason and the mentality of the other partner. Here, a proper counsellor is needed.

What steps can be taken to avoid separation?

These causes can be treated and remedied.

Here are a few things to keep in mind:

- When there are some problems, most of the time it is important that relatives from both sides take a back seat and do not interfere in it. This is the best way out; please understand that our children are trying to re-establish the relationship. Indeed, we can give them advice only if they want it. Unsolicited advice doesn't really help.
- One has to find out whether there is anyone else, besides the partner, under whose influence one partner rejects another partner, for example, friends, some other influential person, or some close relationships.
- Is there a comparison of the partner with one's ideal person like father, mother, or anybody else?
- As a counsellor I haven't come across a perfect husband or a perfect wife. We create an image of our partner in a quality world. Improving upon this image and rearranging the 'quality world' should be done at this stage.
- Misunderstanding or misconception is like a ghost, and we have to drive it out of our life.

- As per our likes and dislikes we have selected our partner. How could our likes go wrong? Do we feel that we have selected the wrong person? Believing in our choices and working on the relationship is the best option rather than to ask for separation.

- Forgive him/her whenever necessary.

- Do not discuss your differences/arguments with anyone else, not even your parents. It has been my observation that small differences between partners are discussed by either or both partners. The other partner feels very hurt by it.

Remedial measures:

- Both partners should accept that there are problems in their togetherness; it is possible to solve them, and this is in their hands.

- Keeping aside the ego, they should examine themselves ruthlessly and find out the fundamental reason for the problems.

- There should be frank communication and that is not for pointing out faults of the partner but for solving the problem. This must be kept in mind in every communication.

- Once the problem is identified it becomes easy to decide what measures should be taken. At this stage others from the same age group, older members of the family, help of a counselor can be useful.

- Whatever measures are suggested, they have to be implemented. If needed, during this period, both could stay away from each other. They need not go to a lawyer or a court for that.

- What if we get a chance to live with each other? Be grateful for this chance. Keep aside the harshness, pride, physical and mental bruises due to quarrels. Consciously put aside the blame hurled at you and the subsequent mental wounds. When we are angry, we are filled with negative emotions and that one word leads to another and we start blaming each other. Try to throw such words out of your mind. In the beginning you may feel that this is not possible but for our own future you can certainly do that. As a relationship takes some time to shape up, more time is required to mend a spoiled, broken relationship because now we are trying to mend and give a good shape to a damaged relationship.
- If the problem is not solved till the sixth step, then expert advice is the only remaining option.

Decision of divorce: right or wrong?

Is it a good idea to ask for separation? That is the question. In such a scenario ask yourself the following questions. You will get the answer yourself.

Question 1

"Do you feel that you are being physically, mentally and sexually exploited and/or abused but can't do anything about it?"

Nobody has any reason or right to exploit or abuse you, therefore, so this should not be tolerated. There are some steps which you can take; but many times, the partner is not ready to accept such measures. In such a situation you must tell the partner firmly and sternly that if he doesn't change his behavior, you will be forced to put an end to the relationship.

Question 2

"Are you forgetting your identity unwillingly? Is your self-esteem or self-worth in your eyes going down in your partner's company?"

Extreme dominance and dictatorial behavior of the partner can endanger your own identity; a feeling of helplessness sets in. You are engrossed in negative thoughts like, 'There will be no more happy moments in my life, I may not be able to live my life the way I want to, I will have to be in this situation till the end.' You forget that you have full right to live life the way you want to live.

Though separation is not the only way out, sometimes you have to take some harsh decisions.

Question 3

"Do you feel that you no more love your partner and now it is impossible for you to accept your partner?"

Consult a counsellor to find out whether a separation can be avoided.

Question 4

"Is there extreme hatred in your mind for the partner? Do you really feel that your choice was based on wrong assumptions?"

Think whether your partner loves you or not. Take professional help if you are confused about your decision.

Question 5

"There are constant quarrels and conflicts, and you are tired of that. Now no more strength is left in you to face the conflicts. Is it that you are completely fed up with staying together? Do you feel that even counseling is not really bringing in any change in the situation?"

Question 6

"Do you think that despite the help or advice of the elders in the family, friends, relatives and counselor, the partner is quite adamant on his/her behavior? Is he/she is going back on the promises and vows as time passes?"

Question 7

"You have sacrificed yourself physically, mentally, and financially in order to make the coexistence successful; do you feel that it is all lost? Do you think that you have the strength to make life better than the one you are living?"

Question 8

"Sexual pleasure is an important aspect of a married life. Are you getting it? If not, did you consult a sexologist?"

Take advice from a doctor or an expert or have an open discussion with your partner to look for options.

Question 9

Assess your readiness for living alone after separation. There is a possibility that you may have another partner. But you have no guarantee that the next relationship will last for a long time. The seekers I work with often prefer to stay together, adjusting, accepting, and adapting to the same relationship fearing to stay alone.

Most important:

The decision to get a divorce must be entirely your own decision. Take advice but think and decide your choice personally because the advisor is not wearing your shoes. He/she or also your parents cannot imagine or understand your suffering, only you know what you are going through and therefore the decision has to be yours and only you have the ability to decide. Quietly ask yourself, "Do you still want to be bound by such togetherness?"

The answer lies with you.

What does your inner voice tell you?

"Do you really want to separate? Do you really want a divorce?" Ask these questions and listen to what your mind tells you. Don't go only by intellect or reason; use the wisdom that you have gathered through experience. Go for self-talk and ask for your own advice. Be honest with your thoughts and with yourself and then decide. Perhaps your decision will be troublesome to you, but it will be your own decision and that will give you strength to face the consequences. Your inner energy will be activated. Perhaps you had forgotten the support system of a job, money, friends, you will see it again. You will see the path to the future. You will believe that the future holds something much better than whatever is left behind; you will bravely opt for the journey to a better future.

And yes, have faith that you do have the required strength in you.

Your separation decision will be right when you think it through.

"Regardless of the situation, I will face loneliness, with no support, I don't wish this relationship to continue. In any case I want to discard first this relationship."

Psychological first aid in separation:

'Before You Find a Counsellor' by Dr Pratibha Deshpande will shed more light on this. Take help from this book.

When wounded, we give first aid to the body; similarly, when the mind is wounded psychological first aid is required. Separation is the most traumatic and unpleasant event in one's life. It affects us in many ways.

Here are the general symptoms:

Physical: Complaints about sleep pattern/ loss of sleep, disturbed digestion like loose motions, nausea, loss of appetite, stomachache, headache.

Emotional: Both the partners go through emotional chaos. It is very painful to realize that the person I loved so much in the past is no longer a part of my life. They have to face a mixture of emotions like fear, anxiety, sorrow, dejection, indifference, apathy, irritation, anger, insensitivity, aloofness, disorder, depression etc. A feeling of loneliness engulfs them. Memories of the past trouble them. They feel guilty and shameful about being separated from the family and blame themselves. The feeling that we are getting separated from society and this adds to their loneliness.

Psychological or mental: Lack of concentration, forgetfulness, unwanted memories deeply rooted in the mind, bad dreams or daydreams, loss of confidence in one's own values and beliefs, problems in communication.

Behavior: Drowning oneself in work or in some addiction, avoiding things, places, people who could remind you of the partner, losing sense of facts, reality, excessive dependence on others or ruling others, carelessness, inattention to others, sometimes being extremely energetic or active.

In such a situation, all they need is an affectionate touch, positive words, mental support, sympathy, and unconditional love. ***They need ABC- Attend to Basic needs with Compassion- from someone.***

Victims who are given psychological first aid are called 'seekers'. Having a dialogue with a seeker and helping him in

gaining mental stability, peace and security is the first aid. If the friends, relatives, family members and colleagues behave consciously, compassionately and lovingly with a seeker, the first aid can give the expected results.

A network of those (friends, relatives, family members and colleagues) that can help a seeker should be formed so that he is constantly kept occupied with something or the other. Then negative thoughts will not enter his mind. In such a situation, consolation has to be given without using words. Gossip has to be completely avoided.

What should the members of this network do?

- Active Listening: Try to motivate him to open up but do not force him. Listen to whatever he says, the steam will be automatically be let out.
- Non-verbal listening: Trying to understand the seeker's meaning beyond words through his body language.
- Translate his words and put them in the proper context, check with him whether that is correct.
- Help him understand his own emotions.
- Try to help him to adopt methods of reducing mental stress and having peace.
- Inspire or encourage him to practice self-help.

Things to remember while giving first aid

During this period both the partners and their close family are mentally hurt. At this time friends, relatives, neighbors should behave in such a way that the afflicted family should not be troubled by them.

Things to do:

- Your intention is to support the seeker. Let him know through your behavior that your attention is concentrated on him.
- Establish a contact with the seeker. Initially have a friendly dialogue with him. Behave kindly and peacefully with him. Create an atmosphere so that he opens up with you.
- Don't make false promises like things will be alright soon.
- Instead, use factually more correct words/sentences like 'I can understand your feelings,' or 'Your flexibility and happy temperament will help you come out of the situation.' These words will be more effective.
- Everyone's way of handling stress is different. It depends on one's experiences. Help the seeker to use his/her own method and respect it.
- Help the seeker to maintain his social and other relations. Give him the right information at the right time.

Avoid these:

- Repeated enquiries about the details of his extremely painful experiences.
- Let him take the lead in conversation; you only listen. Forcing him to give details of whatever has happened.
- Don't make promises that can't be kept or that can't be brought into reality.

Separation, what next?

Something that was going on for a long time is over now. A chapter is closed. A relationship that was formed with many hopes and aspirations is dissolved.

Every separation has its own distinct different story. It could be newly married couples or couples living together who have had

a long relationship, having or not having children, either one or both want the separation-whatever the case may be. There are two opposite emotions that come out of it; one is hurt, and the other is relief.

The period after a separation is very challenging. You are used to living together and now face loneliness; that is a horrible feeling. You are facing emotional storms. The older the relationship, the more the suffering.

It is not easy but it is a chance to search for yourself again. An opportunity to find out the latent source of energy and hidden strengths in you. An opportunity to concentrate on yourself and get ahead in life. A lot of questions confront you.

- How would my life be if I lived alone?
- Where do I want to go?
- What is my destination?
- From where should I begin?
- How will I get the right direction?

Important points to be noted:

- **Express your pain or sorrow;** do not repress it. Recognize your emotions. Accept the facts. While getting married, one always thinks of a happy life together and not of a separation but accept whatever has happened. It is quite natural to feel sorry about your situation or that there is a loss because of your behavior but do not get stuck in that. Think about the positive things that can be filled in the vacuum that is there in your life now.

- **Find a way out of negative emotions and feelings**: Get rid of the baggage of negative feelings from old relationships.

Seek help from someone who has no vested interest or of a counselor. Ask yourself, 'Is it helping me in any way to think about the same things repeatedly?' The answer will be 'No'. Learn to get rid of such thoughts and move ahead. Separation is not the end of life, there is much more to life ahead.

- **Love yourself:** One consequence of a separation could be self-denial, sacrificing own's interests; come out of it and love yourself. The confidence that is lost because of thoughts like 'I went wrong,' or 'Something is lacking in me and that's why this happened,' has to be regained. Recognize your own value and merit. There is a mine of gold hidden in everyone; search for it. Make a list of the qualities and skills that you possess, for example, kindness, generosity etc.

- **Remember how you were earlier:** If you have been married for a long time, it is possible that you have not done many things by now. For example, you like to travel but your partner doesn't. Remember your hobbies, like reading a book, before you got married. Give at least ten minutes for that every day. While entering a new life your responsibilities are going to increase. It is possible that due to stress and tension you may not be able to fulfill them properly. Therefore, drive away the tensions. Learn to laugh at yourself. Forget about the worries of yesterday. Live in the present. Remove the blinkers of your sorrow from your eyes and look around; you will find a lot of things that make you happy.

- **Explore a new aspect of your personality:** Separation is an upsetting incident but there could be a silver lining to it. You can adopt a new lifestyle after separation. Perhaps you can go to a new place, accept a new job and begin a new life. But

please see to it that any change that is made must be conducive to your health and creativity.

- **Walk alone:** Living alone is not living a lonely life. A lot of people live alone. Make acquaintances, friends who share your hobbies and interests. Expand your social boundaries. (This concept is written in detail in 'Swayam 365' by Dr Pratibha Deshpande)

- **Search for a new relationship:** You have lost one inning but that doesn't mean that you cannot play another one. You are not a winner in one game; that cannot be a reason for denying life. Why cuddle mistakes made in the past and be lonely for the entire life? Be honest even with mistakes. Accept your responsibility in them, mend them and begin afresh with a new innings. Life is beautiful, welcome and accept it with open arms.

- **Accept your new role with love:** Ask yourself, what can give me joy? What is the objective of my life? Answers to these two questions will tell you where your happiness lies and guide you towards efforts in the right direction.

- **Listen to your inner voice:** Thoughts have tremendous power. It is likely that your thoughts will be actualized. What you think about, you bring about. Therefore, examine your thoughts. Negative thoughts kill your energy. The positive thought that, hereafter good things are going to happen in your life will increase your energy.

- **Be honest with yourself:** During this period your decision-making ability may be caught in a dilemma. You may have doubts about the rightness/wrongness about what you are doing. Listen to your inner voice in such a situation. If you have doubts, wait for some time. 'Time' is a very good medicine and healer. Go ahead only when you feel that your decision is right.

> **Separation is not the end of our life. We don't have to stay alone for the rest of our life either. Even though two people come together with dreams about life, sometimes their choices can be wrong. There is no stigma associated with separation.**

4

Infidelity

"Can I trust you?" asked the man.
"Can I trust you?" asked the woman.

What is infidelity?

Human beings have always been wanderers and seekers since the beginning of time. Their primitive nature was to roam around as loners or in herds, choosing anyone and anywhere they wanted, for having physical intercourse. Feelings and emotions were not a part of this transaction of physical needs and their fulfilment.

Then, when they became gatherers and formed groups, the thought of taking care of females and children borne by them occurred, and they decided to live in communities, societies. It was then that the concept of monogamy came. Marriage was introduced as a bond which ensured security and safety of kids and their mothers by the males who married them.

As marriage meant monogamy, over a period of time, it became the most dominating feature of society. The bond was

considered sacred and it bound both the male and the female with love, care and respect for each other.

In due course of time, as one of the two partners got attracted to someone else outside of the relationship and made a physical or emotional attachment, it became taboo in this society. The term for this was given as infidelity.

Infidelity has been there since ages, but stayed always hidden under the cover of secrecy, at times put under the rug to avoid the distress, which comes with it.

"Thou shalt not commit adultery" (Exodus 20:14) is one of the Ten Commandments.

Infidelity is a violation of commitment given to your partner in a romantic relationship. It is going beyond the boundary of marriage or romantic relationship where two people had laid the foundation of togetherness with trust, love, and respect to be upheld forever.

It is a breach of trust in a romantic partnership where the sexual act of intimacy, which was exclusive, has been violated.

Probable reasons of infidelity:

Why does one spouse cheat on the other spouse? What happens when one or both of the partners want to cross an unwritten line when a relationship is formed? There are various reasons why a partner may be tempted to cheat. The real reason is known only to both of them or to the one who cheats.

Whatever the reasons are, 'Infidelity' cannot be justified. It is pure cheating on the other partner. It is a 'Breach of promise and trust.'

Generally, the reasons are of two types.

1. Internal
2. External.

Internal causes are:

- Emotional vulnerability, emotional inability, emotional turbulence, low or high emotional competence, low self-esteem, insecurities, fear of commitment, child abuse, child trauma, lack of emotional connection in relationships, bad parenting, feeling inadequate, boredom, dissatisfaction, failure, sexual dissatisfaction in marriage, unresolved past issues, desire for independence, just for thrill are some of the causes.
- The quality world image of partner is different from the real partner.
- Psychological trauma or mental trauma.
- Sex addiction.
- Sexual opportunism.
- Multiple partners for sex.
- Childhood physical abuse.

There are many more reasons that are linked to personality. There is no problem in saying that this is a kind of disease. It can, however, be cured by medical treatment.

External causes are:

1. Unavailability of one partner.
2. Lack of communication.
3. No emotional support.
4. Midlife crises.
5. Adding spice in life or notorious nature.

6. lack of sexual pleasure.

7. Long distance relationship:

Infidelity, a two-way sword:

No matter what the reasons are for infidelity, there is always a drift in relationships after the act of infidelity.

Infidelity is said to be a two-way sword that not only brings happiness but also guilt, fear, and trauma. It is seen that the couple, no matter how much they try to make amends, always experience shame lingering on between them.

It brings with it a lot of traumas too. The cheating partner, firstly, is in constant fear of being caught which causes sleepless nights. The initial excitement, which once gave joy, later starts giving discomfort. When the partner comes to know what has been happening behind his or her back, then there is utter turmoil. If children are involved, things can get bad for them too. The ultimate choice of forgiving the partner or taking separation should be in the hands of the couple only.

Story of double betrayal:

There was a loving relationship between Siya and Samar. They had been in love for a year and wanted to get married. Siya was an IT professional and earned well. Samar was her boss in the company. Siya constantly told Samar to let her meet his family and to meet hers now, and they should get married. In the office everyone looked at her with a feeling of dislike, but no one confronted her for anything. She thought that maybe they were jealous of her as she could be their boss's wife soon. It was one day that Liza, in her office,

called her and told her the truth about Samar. She told her that he was already married and that he had a family in Canada. Siya did not believe it but when she confronted Samar, he confessed that it was true. Siya's world shattered; she did not know what to do. Samar had cheated not only on her, but his wife too. She first thought she would inform his wife but then realized that she was also at fault and what about kids? So, she stayed quiet but withdrew herself from Samar and even left the job later. She made the right choice, but it took her a long time to recover from the trauma.

General Effects of infidelity:

- Infidelity breaks the hearts of both the partners in one way or the other.
- There is an element of uncertainty, once infidelity creeps in.
- Past and future both are at stake.
- Families are disturbed.
- The trauma caused at times is way more than it appears.

Effects on the one who has been cheated upon:

The act of infidelity brings with it a plethora of effects upon the partner who has been cheated. Let us discuss some of these here:

- The partner starts to feel foolish for not being able to see the act happening in front of his or her eyes. He or she blames his or her own self many times.
- He or she feels that there is something lacking in himself or herself because of which the partner has cheated.

- It brings the feeling of anger which is so deep rooted in this situation that it can cause the person to develop anger issues in the long run.
- At times, the partner who has been cheated upon feels helpless, especially if dependent financially upon the other.
- A hatred also develops both towards one's own self and the partner, who has cheated. The extent of initial trauma can be so wide, that the partner loses all emotional and mental stability.
- The ability to trust another person again or the same person, if forgiven, does not develop easily.
- The knot that comes in the soft woven tapestry of the relationship, once broken cannot be remade.

It is seen that the hurt is so deep for the one who is cheated upon that he or she may take years or even a lifetime to recover or forget the hurt and pain cost.

If children are involved, then the partner feels so worthless because the children suffer an unstable situation caused by this trauma.

Effects on both the partners:

- The breach of trust in infidelity is often never recovered. Partners may not want to reconcile until there is financial, emotional, spiritual, or social pressure.
- Both the partners are affected emotionally and mentally. The partner who cheats feels guilty and the other partner takes every single opportunity to make them feel ashamed. The partner who has been cheated upon has the choice to forgive and forget, to move on with or without the relationship.

- Some couples may choose to stay together but live independent lives. This is when there is a choice made by the one who has been cheated upon and he or she does not want to make mockery of himself or herself by going in for separation.
- Some choose to stay together and the partner who has been cheated upon holds an upper hand in decisions of family as a punishment to the one who has cheated. Public humiliation is a major factor because of which couples may choose to stay together.
- Involvement of children in these decisions is also seen when the effect is on the whole family, not just the two people in the relationship.

Effects of infidelity on family:

Infidelity not only affects the partners but also their families. If children are there, they may get distressed, and one may set a wrong example for their children. It may affect the child's mental health and eventually his or her future. If their parents come to know about the infidelity it may affect their health also. They may question themselves about their way of bringing up their child, and it may be very difficult for them to face society. This brings a lot of anguish, hatred, and disappointment among the elders.

Infidelity may also result in a child born out of wedlock. The child's future is at stake. The law in our country is very strong and the illegitimate child does not have any right in property. What's the fault of the child for the mistake made by the adults?

Case 1:

Story of Forgiveness

Saurabh and Dipti were a happily married couple. There had been ten years of marriage in which Dipti had undergone a lot of trouble with in-laws but now was doing fine, as she kept fighting back in every situation that came along her way. She was working also and took care of her family very well. Saurabh was very proud of her but did not support her much when it came to issues related to his mother. They had two lovely kids, and she was raising them very well. Saurabh was very successful in his career and even travelled a lot. He went on national and international tours a lot. A high post, a handsome salary, no responsibility of kids (as Dipti handled kids), travel to various beautiful destinations, slowly Saurabh became very distan from Dipti.

All of a sudden on a Saturday morning, as Dipti checked her phone to see her mails, she got the biggest shock of her life. There were pics and messages from an unknown number in which Saurabh was with another lady in a compromising state. Dipti had tears in her eyes and was also scared also. Anger filled her lungs instead of air. She also felt lost and did not understand what to do, whom to tell, whether to confront Saurabh or not.

It was then that she called that number and a male voice answered. He told Dipti that Saurabh was having an affair with his wife and that he had caught them. He also told her that the chats were a proof along with photos. He

said that he could give more proof and asked Dipti to speak to Saurabh.

Dipti confronted Saurabh but he refused saying that the man was trying to fix all this so that he could get a divorce from his wife, who was Saurabh's friend. He told that for the past few months he was talking to her, but there was nothing more. But his eyes and body language were saying something else. Dipti was a Human Resource professional and knew very well when someone was lying. She knew Saurabh was lying but she chose to agree with him and did not make it into a big issue. Saurabh said that he had met this female after years and they were just talking. He promised not to speak to her again and to be more present for her and their family.

In her heart Dipti forgave him because she did not want to make it difficult for her kids. But she could not trust Saurabh again. She kept on checking his phone, mail and messages. It became traumatic for her. Though she had forgiven him, she was not sure if she would ever be normal. It took years for her to fully recover from it, but she saved her marriage and now they are a happy family.

Dipti chose to forgive him and move forward. It was difficult, but she saved the sinking ship!

From the perspective of a counsellor:

- At such a time, the key question arises whether to forgive or not.
- Forgiving a spouse who has betrayed is not easy.
- Winning trust again is a difficult task.
- Forgiveness can lead to extreme suffering in life.

- Even in small quarrels, this issue rears its head again and again.
- The other partner does not leave an opportunity to mentally torture the partner who has been unfaithful. In the end, the person comes to a decision to separate rather than die every day.
- This is a crucial time for both partners.
- This situation takes many years to resolve.
- But if the unfaithful spouse is truly remorseful, it is best to forgive.

In such cases, taking the help of a counselor can bring the situation under control as they know how to handle each partner in this and teach both the partners accordingly.

Case 2:

When forgiving is not the choice

Kabir and Arpita were married by their parents' choice as it was an arranged marriage. After marriage Kabir got a promotion and was transferred to California. They both moved there and started a new life. A new city and a new life… it's challenges and adjustments made it difficult for Arpita initially, but then she adjusted.

It was a year later that she conceived and shared the news of her pregnancy with their family and friends. It was again not so easy as they were alone there, and she had to take care of the house and herself and this kept her tired all the time. It so happened that their physical relations got disturbed. Kabir tried but his physical needs were now

taking a toll over him. They were both young and did not know how to handle such things. Due to some complications, doctor has advised Kabir to refrain from sex.

As this was happening, Kabir met a girl in his office who was young and beautiful. She was his secretary, Liza. She was a smart woman, loving, affectionate and caring by nature. They both started sharing their days together and with work, they also shared their personal life. Their friendship developed and gradually it crossed the line of friendship and Kabir formed a physical relationship with Liza.

He did not realize how time changed his relationship with his wife. All this while, Arpita was fighting her struggles with pregnancy and managing everything herself at the home front. It was then that she realized something was amiss in her marriage these days. She asked Kabir if there was something troubling him, he did not say anything. Nine months passed and Arpita delivered a baby girl. Her parents and Kabir's parents, both came to visit them and after forty days when they went back, she hired a nanny for her baby. She started making efforts to come close to Kabir, but he told her it was ok and that she should first be absolutely alright.

It was then that she called Liza and asked if all was good at the office. She was told that all was fine. She still felt something was there and decided to find it on her own. She then picked up Kabir's phone and checked it, but it was locked. She asked for the password, and he refused. She confronted him strongly this time and said that she wanted

to know the truth if something was happening in his life which she did not know.

He again told her nothing was wrong. A year passed but there was no physical contact between them. It was now very difficult for Arpita to handle. She told her mother about this, and they immediately came to meet her. She explained to them the full situation and they confronted Kabir. It was then that he said that he had been with another woman for the past two years and that he was sorry for what has happened.

Arpita's world collapsed but she held herself strong and asked for a divorce.

She did not forgive him. She wished him the best for his life but decided to move back to her parents and start afresh.

From a perspective of a counsellor:

- Did Arpita make the right decision? Yes!
- Why is the decision right? He didn't tell the truth after she asked him many times, he kept cheating on her, at that time he only saw his own happiness.
- He showed no patience when Arpita was struggling with her pregnancy. The child belonged to both, at that time it was his duty to take responsibility of Arpita and keep her happy.
- This disloyalty did not happen once. There was no mistake in the sentiment. There is no forgiveness for this because even if he repents now, what is the guarantee that he will not behave like this again in his life?

Seeing such cases makes one feel numb. Do you think these children were not taught patience? One mistake can be

understood, but one who makes repeated mistakes becomes a criminal. A lot of good can come from coming to a counselor with the realization that one is making a mistake.

I remember two cases:

1. Santosh came for counseling on his own. "Doctor, there are some mistakes that I want to stop. I want to treat it."

2. Ananya comes and says, "I am addicted to sex, can you get me out of it?"

In these two cases, there could be corrections.

Many cases are treatable. Internalized infidelity is a psychological problem that is treatable. Adultery, due to this reason, can also be resolved if dealt with in time. But time is very important. Once time passes, the situation is more likely to escalate.

So, we can say that forgiving the partner or not, loving him or her anymore, staying in the relationship or leaving it, whatever the decision has to be made, it has to be done by the partners themselves

as it affects them the most. Others can give suggestions, advice or hope but the actual battle post the decision is for the partners.

Care to be taken by both partners:
- Give enough time to your relationship.
- Don't be so careless and neglect signs, that you don't even notice that the relationship is deteriorating.
- Respect your partner's wish.
- Listen to your partner when he or she is trying to tell you something.
- It is very important to talk openly with each other.

If you want to maintain this relationship for a long time, choose to stay away from infidelity. This is an earnest request. If such lust occurs, treat it immediately, seek the help of a counsellor. If your partner makes a mistake, forgive him by extending the boundaries of your trust. If you want to have a long-distance relationship, be careful before problems arise. Talk openly with your partner before you become disillusioned.

Section

5

Tunes That Touch the Heart

1. Physical Intimacy

2. A Miracle of Love

1

Physical Intimacy

Physical intimacy shouldn't define anyone, it should be a part of who we are, what we feel about ourselves and how we see ourselves from within this body. We must know that sex is something we do but sexuality is something that makes us what we are, not just physically but mentally and spiritually.

In doing so we must understand that sex is an act which takes place to fulfill our physical needs, but our sexuality takes us deeper into our own self. Thus, knowing that our body, mind and soul, all are equally important and must be taken into consideration just as any other aspect of our life.

Human life has four main goals or aims: Dharma, Artha, Kama, and Moksha. Purushartha is the object of human pursuit when they are combined. Dharma is morality, Artha is prosperity, Kama is love and pleasure and Moksha is spiritual value. The love that binds two minds and two bodies should grow stronger as they come closer to each other. Complete surrender to each other leads to ultimate closeness of mind and body. When a love life

is filled with concern and passion, intimacy is a pleasure beyond description.

Among all living things, food, fear, sleep, and sex are the most important and inevitable instincts.

Along with physical, biological, emotional, and behavioral components, sexuality includes an important component of rationality. Sex is a basic human need and serves as a drive for personal fulfilment and for the perpetuation of species. Sexuality refers to all feelings, attitudes and activities related to sex.

The issue of sexuality has always been one of curiosity, debate, repression, and aggression. Contradictions and contrasts have marked the subject. A cultural and social context, as well as economic and political ideologies, affect values and beliefs about sexuality.

Even though sex and all facets related to it were once viewed as dirty and private, today's society is gradually shifting its views on sexuality due to the fast pace of change in all of society. Though sex may be forbidden for open discussion in the Indian family setting, there is more openness in communication about sexuality among various family members and friends nowadays.

There is a lot of awareness and motivation towards this aspect of an individual because society is developing, getting modernized and wants a healthy environment for everyone when it comes to sexuality.

Dimensions of sexuality include social, cognitive, emotional, and ethical perspectives. These aspects deeply affect our day-to-day lives, and we need to be aware of them. As we know, sexual attraction between individuals mainly of opposite sexes, has been the basis of perpetuation of species since times immemorial.

Ones' perception of self as a sexual being and others' perception of individuals' sexuality are important dimensions affecting intimate relations between two sexually involved individuals.

Physical intimacy between couples:

Physical intimacy forms not only an important dimension towards the development of couple relationships, actually, it is the basis for couple relationships. Romantic relationship between two persons belonging to different sexes, involving a social, religious, or civil ceremony is generally the rule in India for formation of couple relationships. However, in a diverse cultural and religious milieu like India, there exist some other patterns of sexual bond formation which include premarital relations, extramarital relations, live-in relationships and in the present generation, homosexual relations.

In a relationship, it is given to understand that the man and the woman must be able to satisfy their sexual needs and desires. Sexuality is often used as a powerful tool by the two partners to determine power positions and get the other person to agree on certain issues.

In India, there is a general disapproval of the erotic aspect of life. The sexual code of conduct for the partner endorses the expectation that physical love and passion are shame-ridden affairs and these should be performed only during couple's private moments.

For example:

Rahan and Tina, a married couple for five years, were filing for separation. They were sent to a counsellor and upon a detailed discussion with Tina, the counsellor found

out that their sexual life was not satisfying. Tina being a girl of desires and aspirations also had a want for happiness in her sex life. Who else would she ask for? Tina said that during the act Rahan only focused on his satisfaction and out of ten times she only got pleasure two times. The remaining eight times she told the counsellor that she felt used. She also expressed her concern that when she tried to explain this to Rahan he said, "I can't be focusing on how you feel. For me it's an act of physical satisfaction." He was then sent to sexuality counsellor where he understood that sexual pleasure was for both the partners and not just about himself. Upon developing this understanding, their marriage was saved and now both enjoy pleasure together.

A healthy relationship requires physical intimacy. In addition to strengthening their bond, it can also bring them closer together. Physical intimacy releases endorphins, which can reduce stress and anxiety. In addition, it can help boost a person's self-esteem and create a sense of security in their relationship. However, it has been distorted in many ways.

Understanding the balance created by sexual act

In coitus, two bodies unite with the intention of pleasing each other. This is a sacred act. There is a cohesion of feelings, emotions, thoughts, and pleasure. The broader picture that we have in front of us is completely different. Rather than satisfying the emotional yearning, the act of union is performed hurriedly to satisfy physical lust. We fail to recognize that the ability to unite is one of the greatest gifts the 'creator' has given us. As for its physical and spiritual power, we are unable to gauge its depth. If we keep a few things in mind, we can make our marriage happy and perfectly balanced.

When in marriage communion takes place, it is to create perfect harmony between the two newly-united beings, not just at a bodily but at a soul level. When in such a state of balance, a child is conceived, it generates a harmonious character in that child too.

Sexuality

The open discussion of *'Sex to Spirituality'* by a high intellectual like Osho is wrongly criticized. For the average person, sex is a form of extended lust or distortion, whereas spirituality is the highest form of retirement from all pleasures of life. Sexuality and spirituality are wrongly viewed as opposing concepts.

Today's generation seems to understand many terms better than previous generations. They have realized the difference between anticipating and remaining concerned. After performing an act, they take responsibility with maturity. They do not dwell on unnecessary ifs and buts. No topic is off limits or banned for them. There is no doubt that they have strong opinions and clear ideas about sex, intimacy, virginity, vices, virtues, and so forth. We are astonished by their knowledge and thoughtfulness.

'What' they want and 'why' they want is clear to them. We do not care if they are 'rightfully wrong' or 'wrongfully right.'

To date, virginity has been considered a 'must' aspect. However, today's youth do not seem to think so. 'Virginity' has become a bookish concept for many of them.

Another extensively debated issue is whether they should practice intimacy before getting into a legal relationship. Nevertheless, we must realize and respect the space that each of us strives and wishes for. Let's focus on 'physical intimacy' for now and its importance in a couple.

Intimacy is the topic we are discussing here, but it is not the same as sex counselling. As a result of the discussion, you will be able to appreciate the importance of intimacy. When having difficulty getting intimate on a physical or emotional level, it is best to consult a sexologist.

Both man and woman differ in physical, emotional, intellectual, and mental levels. They have unlike expectations. Intimacy will be fruitful and satisfactory only when they both realize the differences and acknowledge them earnestly. When two minds come together, the connection is deeper. Naturally, intercourse becomes extremely pleasurable under such circumstances.

Sex is a two-way feeling; it is not a one-sided track. Satisfaction of both the partners is equally important. Lust of one and reluctance of another cannot be called as an act of intimacy. It is cruelty or utter selfishness.

Sex is an art to be explored carefully and lovingly. Only then will love-making satisfy both the partners.

Responsibility of partner in the sexual act

Remember that woman is shy by nature. In addition, she has been compelled to play the submissive role for ages. Hence, she is unable to express her desires. She has been taught to suppress the most basic urges like hunger and interest. Then, who would care to listen to her about her 'sex instincts?' Apart from many other issues, the Indian family set-up makes it difficult for couples to have privacy. Hence, it is really very hard for a couple to have some relaxing moments to understand each other before actual intimate act.

To make the 'lovemaking' enjoyable, memorable, and pleasurable a few basic things that one should keep in mind are a

clean and airy bedroom, a calm and peaceful mind, a stress-free and eager attitude, and readiness to seek the level of intimacy the partner desires. It is true that the physical bodies in the act cannot be changed, but motivation, readiness and interest should be maintained. Touch should be respected and adored. Willingness should be welcomed. Understanding the partner's needs and fulfilling them should be the priority, especially that of the woman. Generally, a woman would not openly admit or express her wishes and desires. So, those should be particularly on the priority list of her partner. He should make special efforts to give her satisfaction.

Sex has tremendous power. If the lust part becomes overpowering, then sex becomes just an act which might not satisfy the partner or sometimes which would hurt the partner. On the other hand, when intimacy is lined with love, caring, and sharing, then love-making results in increased faith. Such partnership is fruitful to both the spouses. They come together not as a part of life or a ritual, instead they are eager to be in each other's company. Apart from the physical need, they crave for each other as they care deeply. Attraction is a natural phenomenon but so is distraction. But true love holds them together without compulsion.

As the urge to have intercourse is very natural it should never be suppressed. But that does not mean that lovemaking should be the only thing on one's mind. Control means a lot and is essential as well. Moreover, when the partner does not desire the act of intercourse then it should not be forcibly done. A healthy relationship will always respect the 'no' when the partner refuses.

Types of sexuality

Some common labels have been given to people to use to identify their sexuality. These labels are not necessarily to define

about who they are going to have sex with, but it is about how they feel and how they choose to identify themselves.

- **Straight or heterosexual**- these are the people who are attracted mostly to people of the opposite sex or gender.
- **Gay or homosexual**- these are the people who are mostly attracted to the people of the same sex or gender.
- **Lesbian**- these are the women who are attracted to the same gender.
- **Pan sexual**- these are the people who are attracted to romantic and sexual partners of any gender or sexual identity.
- **Poly sexual**- these are attracted to romantic and sexual partners of many but not all genders or sexuality.
- **Asexual** - these are the people who do not experience sexual attraction and/or do not desire to act on sexual attractions.

Sex-related problems

Some of us may have some sex-related problems, not just on a physical level but on emotional or psychological level. The roots may be hidden in childhood. A child, especially a girl-child, must bear unwanted/abusive touches from a very early age in life. Being a female worsens the intensity of sexual abuse quite a lot. Such a girl is unable to express her fear. She is not allowed to speak and if she does so, nobody believes her. Rather, she is blamed for being provocative. However horrible is the feeling and experience of touch and fear, she alone must pull on. It's a fact that girls are abused at the hands of their own relatives, including their own fathers. With due respect to all caring and loving fathers, let us accept this truth. Naturally, a girl who has experienced the first 'male touch' under ugly circumstances would always consider lovemaking as a vice or horrible thing to do. From the small number of metro

women that we see around us, we cannot conclude that 'all is well' in our society.

On the contrary, sex is an avoided topic, it's taboo to talk about it. Fear, ignorance, shyness, anxiety, etc. are all closely related to women in general. It is very important to drive away any negativity regarding 'sex'. If needed, an expert's guidance should be sought. It should not be delayed due to coyness.

Movies are very much responsible for portraying an incorrect and fancy picture about love and courtship. When in daily life, one fails to experience it, naturally the person experiences depression. Earlier, pornography material was limited. But, with growing internet use and the easily available free sites, everything is simply accessible to each and all. If used wisely, the internet is the best teacher. But that does not happen. Still, despite so much availability, many are unaware of what and how 'lovemaking' is done exactly. Ignorance and lack of proper guidance/training are the main issues.

It is essential to know the 'how' and 'what' of lovemaking prior to marriage. The misleading advertisements in newspapers are harmful. Instead, a sex-counsellor's aid should be sought. Being sexually healthy is our duty and expecting our sex partner to be sexually healthy is our right. Hence, we should make specific efforts in this direction.

Unprotected sex may lead to pregnancy. Termination of pregnancy is a crime. It also shatters a person to the core. It affects emotionally, physically, financially, and, of course, ethically. It may prove to be dangerous to the would-be mother. She may develop problems during termination which might make it difficult for her

to conceive in the later years. So, it is better to take care. Apart from pregnancy, such sex may lead to venereal diseases.

We all have a right to have a pleasant 'love-life'. One may have had a bad experience or a series of such experiences. Yet, it does not mean that everything in life is ugly. With new faith and hope, we should walk hand in hand with our partner. Love and lovemaking have immense power. It is not just physical satisfaction of bodily desires. It requires confidence and eagerness to please our partner. It helps to reach heights, achieve success, and concentrate well. People who are happy, satisfied, pleased, and contented with their sex-life are often successful people. They lead a satisfactory life on a physical, mental, emotional, and intellectual level. They love their partner, are aware of their responsibilities, enjoy the art and act of love making and care for their partner. Such love naturally brings them together on a different level. The sex-energy in such cases allows them to progress on the path of spirituality and gratification. While satisfying this most basic needs, such a couple surely reaches spirituality through sex.

The information that we have shared here is mostly portrayed from the psychological point of view. We are not sex experts, neither do we have expertise in the field of medicine. If anyone is having any sex-related problem or issue, then it is better to seek timely medical advice.

The key to happiness is faith in the partner and one's own self as well.

Case study:

Karthik and Alisha had been married for five years when they sought counseling. After talking with them, it became

apparent that they had had very little or almost no physical contact for the last two years.

"Kartik, why are you so reluctant to get physical in your case? What is the reason for this?" the counsellor asked.

"Don't know."

Elisha's answer was the same.

How could a young couple of thirty or thirty-five years old be so reluctant about something so beautiful?

The next session revealed a few things.

At the age of seventeen, Karthik had a five-year physical relationship with a girl before their marriage.

There were multiple relationships for Alisha before their marriage.

From a perspective of a counsellor:

This is a common trend in the modern generation. I deal with similar cases almost every day.

1. Intimacy at an immature age affects the mind and body.
2. Break ups are quite traumatic.
3. After breaking up, first one relationship, then another relationship is added to forget the pain. After breaking up for the first time, the second relationship happens and the third relationship is added to forget the pain of the second break.
4. It has become a practice in the current era that every relationship involves physical intimacy. (This is my experience after handling so many cases.)
5. Physical intimacy never comes alone. There is also emotional intimacy involved. A physical relationship involves not only the body, but also the mind.

6. Exposure to physical pleasure at an early age inspires the mind to seek it out again. Relationships can be difficult to form if there is a lack of commitment and attachment. Broken promises and short-lived relationships can also make it difficult to trust a partner in the future.

7. In a break up, one experiences a sense of emptiness because emotional trauma drains them.

8. To come out of trauma, one needs proper guidance. To heal from emotional pain, one must take some time for self-love and self-care.

9. In student life, it is important to concentrate on education, career building and becoming emotionally, socially and spiritually strong.

10. When romantic relationships and physical intimacy occur at a young age, they are not mature enough to understand the consequences and this can lead to unstable, unhealthy relationships in the future. There is a sense of guilt, shame, and confusion. Self-esteem and body image can also be negatively affected by early relationships.

11. This can result in depression, anxiety, stress, substance abuse (smoking, drinking, drugs). This may also lead to difficulty in forming future relationships.

12. Having multiple partners and physical relationships with them can make it difficult to maintain attraction after marriage and losing love and intimacy can lead to divorce. The result can also be infidelity and dishonesty, which can negatively impact the marriage.

The same thing happened in this case,

In their student days, Alisha and Karthik experienced physical pleasure. Due to the breakup, both suffered mental trauma. Traces of their emotional turmoil are still lying in their subconscious mind; they still carry the wounds of each of their breakups. It took Alisha and Kartik several sessions to resolve this issue.

Case study:

Parvati came for counseling crying.

"My husband cheated on me. I found out yesterday that he has been having an affair for the last twelve years."

"How did you know?"

"I read his message. For the past few days, I had doubts. I caught him yesterday."

"Then? Did you ask him?"

"Yes. At first, he denied, but then he said that it was true and he loved that girl!"

"Twelve years, a big period and you didn't notice! His touch, his speech, nothing gave you any indication?"

She kept silent. Then she cried and said, "We have had no physical intimacy for twelve years."

"Why?"

"I was on bed rest after my second child was born."

"How many years?"

"Six months."

"Later?"

"We didn't become close."

"Was it your initiative or his?"

"From both."

"There was no discussion, no talking about this subject between the two of you?"

"No!"

"A disgruntled husband?"

"Not at all. Our life was going well. Trips, eating out, shopping, child's school, studies. Our life was going on smoothly."

"My dear girl, this is an important aspect of marriage. You should have realized that he wasn't resentful towards you. You could have taken the help of a doctor."

She was silent, just crying. He had escaped from her hands. He had found his way.

The result was divorce.

From the perspective of a counsellor:

- Ignoring signals.
- It's a staunch reality that all the signs and signals are always there in front of us but we bypass or overlook them.
- It all looks rock solid from outside but is unanchored when seen from inside.

"If your body seeks a relationship, we call it sexuality. If your mind seeks a relationship, it is called companionship. If your emotions seek a relationship, we call it love. If your energies seek a relationship, we call it yoga." Sadguru.

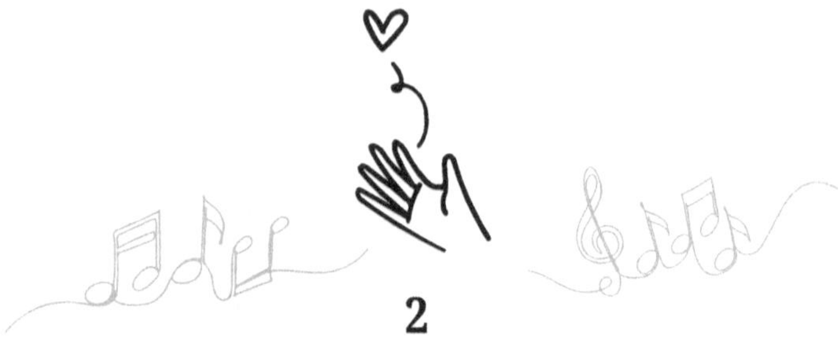

2

A Miracle of Love

Being truly loved and cherished can bring immense joy and happiness. True happiness can be achieved through unconditional love. There is no end to love. People have experienced it differently from generation to generation. The theme of love is prevalent in many classics, stories, poems, dramas, and movies. Nevertheless, everyone feels that his love is unique. The essence of life is love, not food.

Giving takes precedence over receiving or expecting in love. It is possible to destroy a relationship if one fails to give to it. A good relationship can be destroyed by a lack of unconditional giving. The power and limitations of love are often misunderstood. Sadly, we view love as a mutually beneficial arrangement. Many people mistakenly believe that just saying "I love you" fulfils their social, financial, and emotional needs.

What is love?

A feeling of love is like a tiny feather floating lightheartedly. Sight, sound, fragrance, and touch are the languages of love.

Faith in love is never-ending, but it is not blind. Belief in his intentions, respect for your partner›s thoughts and self-esteem is the essence of love. As well as accepting qualities, love also accepts differences and shortcomings.

The benefits of loving your partner will be enjoyed by you and your partner as a result of an earnest and consistent effort.

While loving ourselves, we should not be self-centered. Our ‘self’ should not be forgotten while we love others. Walking on the path of love will be an enjoyable experience with such a balance. Loyalty, mutual trust, conviction, sincerity, and transparency are the characteristics of love.

It is not enough to like someone who is instrumental in arousing love for you to call it love.

There is more to love than physical attraction. Physical attraction may sometimes be the first step to love. However, it may not always lead to love.

- When a physical attraction ends, love may disappear.
- There is no such thing as temporary love. The chemical processes of the brain are closely related to love, according to science. Even today's evolutionary species exhibit the instinct to care for and protect what they have.
- While love is neither mad nor blind, it can bring about a positive change in the lives of those who are deprived as well as those who are unnaturally inclined.
- There is no such thing as infatuation or temptation in love.
- It is love that makes us strong, not love that makes us weak.
- Rather than taking us away from our loved ones, love brings us closer to them.

- There can be no harm in love. The loved ones will never be harmed by it.
- When two people love each other, they become self-sufficient rather than dependent on each other.
- Love is a divine power, not a trivial matter. People are inspired by the words of love.
- Love does not require sacrifice, nor does it require submissiveness or exploitation.
- Love is not a compulsion, but it is a powerful force. Transparency is not captivity. It is a pure and clean feeling, not even a dictatorship, but an ambrosia of delicacy. It is not an injustice, but a way to achieve compatibility.
- We cannot dictate our own terms, nor can we boss our partner around in love.

Love is not about claiming ownership or rights. Love is not a simple exchange of feelings without being accounted for.

Love and the human brain

It is undeniable that love brings us a lot of happiness. We are happy when we fall in love, but we are unaware that this is nature's game designed to create progeny and ensure human survival. We fall in love because of an interaction between many attractive chemicals in our brain. We are victims of nature's sweet plan.

Helen Fischer says that the three stages of love may be related to three chemicals present.

Stage 1: Lust

The secretion of two hormones, testosterone, and estrogen, stimulates the brain and increases sexual desire during this stage.

Stage 2: Attraction

When we are trapped in love, it is a wonderful time. It is as if we are blind and cannot see anything except love. Scientists believe that this stage is caused by the release of three neurotransmitters- adrenaline, dopamine, and serotonin.

The level of adrenaline and cortisol in the blood increases at the beginning of love. Therefore, when we face the person we love, we sweat and have a dry mouth and our heart beats faster.

In love, the brain secretes excessive amounts of dopamine. This state of mind is described as 'Desire and Reward' i.e., the desire to gain pleasure from fulfilling a desire for love. The state of mind is similar to that after consuming drugs like cocaine. Increased dopamine increases sleep and appetite and causes great happiness in small things arising from this new relationship.

The most important hormone is serotonin. Why do we keep thinking about that particular person when we fall in love with him? When we fall in love, does our thinking change? This was the subject of an experiment conducted by Dr. Donatella Marzetti in Pisa. It was deduced that the serotonin levels in the blood of those in love were equal to the lower level of serotonin in the blood of those people who suffered from the mental disorder - 'obsessive-compulsive disorder (OCD)'.

In this step, lovers feel that their love relationship is very different from others. These people enter the next phase of love with a colourful picture of life.

Stage 3: Attachment

Attachment is caused by oxytocin and vasopressin. Couples are inspired to stay together until their children are born and

nurtured. It acts as an agent to create romantic relationships between couples and mother-child relationships.

Vasopressin is also known as an anti-diuretic hormone. During a study of prairie voles, which live in graveyards in Central America, this hormone was found to be active. This hormone strengthens the bond between spouses.

Love between romantic partners:

The four elements of love provide a strong foundation for love.

- Intimacy
- Cohesion
- Commitment
- Passion: feelings and desires that lead to physical attraction, romance, and sexual pleasures

An important aspect of marriage is the commitment to staying together in harmony. The feeling of commitment is being one with your partner and his goals. Through inclusive thinking, 'I' becomes 'we'. The combined energy created by coordination and companionship between partners is greater than the sum of their individual energies. The term 'synergy' refers to this special energy.

Preconditions like ifs and buts are detrimental to love. The rule, 'tit for tat' does not hold good in a relation of love. True love is based on the most important rule of 'giving'.

But unfortunately, marriages are treated as a gainful business, and we start looking forward to receiving benefits in return. Marriage is not a business partnership. If one of them sacrifices something, he need not talk about it; the other partner should understand it. Love should be felt without its expression in words. Marriage is not made up of business partners but companions. There should be no accounting of what has been received against

what one has given. Marriage is not a limited company. It is a nest of affection: a castle of the husband and wife. Strong marriages are based on the foundation of trust in each other. Both are responsible for strengthening this and creating and shaping a good family, nurturing and caring for their children and making them capable of flying high. This is not an easy task, but if both do it together wholeheartedly, it is not that difficult.

Two Milestones in a Partner's Life
- Romantic love
- Mature love

1.   Romantic love

There is nothing more magical, a miracle, madness, or intoxicating than romantic love. We revolve our world around the person we love, when we fall in love. The rest of the world takes a back seat. Nothing seems impossible when you are in love.

What is the reality? A person who falls in love and a person who is intoxicated by alcohol have similar brain functions. Consequently, people in love should not be taken seriously when they make tall claims.

The feeling of falling in love is euphoric. 'I've lost my heart to....' may be one of the many expressions used. There is a feeling of sublime happiness associated with this feeling.

In the first one or two years of marriage, couples experience romantic love. Neither cares about the world's opinion, nor does it matter to them since both are very passionate about love.

People in love hate criticism and consider unsolicited advice to be a form of evil. Their state of mind prevents them from accepting

any suggestions. Getting married during this period is more likely to go wrong. At this stage, love looks like a sweet dream, life looks like a fairy tale, expectations are unrealistic, life without the partner seems impossible, and even the partner's negative qualities seem appealing. Love like this is madness. When the brain is under the influence of a substance, it behaves as though it is intoxicated. Within a year or two, this type of love disappears. Only intimacy and cohesiveness are considered as factors of love in this case. People who want to enter into a love marriage are always advised to proceed with caution in this regard by wise authors.

Even if a person is sure about his love, one should never forget that hormones influence a person's brain when they fall in love. As a result, he ignores the partner's vulnerable qualities. People in love will take realistic decisions with both eyes open, if this awareness is created.

If one is in such a position, he or she should not hesitate to seek advice from elders or from people one trusts. "Ek duje ke liye" shows a very practical strategy. A couple in love should be completely disconnected from each other for six months to a year. Direct visits, phone calls, e-mails, SMS, or friends should not be maintained at all.

If the feeling of love persists after this break, it is real love. We are not against love marriages, of course. A love marriage may prove to be a good start to a beautiful relationship if handled properly with the maturity and dedication required in a sound relationship. It's a great opportunity for partners to get to know each other better. Sometimes, due to lack of maturity and dedication, love marriages have a higher divorce rate than arranged marriages.

2. Mature Love

Immature love says, "I love you because I need you." Mature love says, "I want you because–I love you." Matured love ensures a lifetime commitment, whereas immature love ensures fun. A successful marriage requires mature love. It is impossible for such loving partners to imagine connecting with anyone else. Their belief is that they can only be truly happy and content in each other's company. Getting such love is easier than maintaining it. Constant effort is needed.

Matured love has the following characteristics:

- It is not necessary to change the spouse, as he/she is accepted 'as is'.
- The relationship is balanced, but there is no consensus on everything.
- When planning for the future, there is no fear or doubt.
- Even if opinions differ, there is no dispute.
- Saying 'I love you' is not necessary. Eyes are a way to express love.
- Relationships are based on trust and assurance.
- There is no envy or jealousy at all.

A couple should realize that only romantic love cannot form a strong foundation for living together, but many other factors should also be taken into account. The "one reason" for a successful relationship is not only "love". It is one of several factors. Other factors that must be considered are your spouse's intellectual, emotional, social, spiritual, and physical connection. Relationships between partners do not develop automatically; they need to be built purposefully.

As love matures, it ceases to be purely romantic. There is a strong realization that love must be developed. It is important to consider many things consciously and deliberately. A mature love requires factors such as cooperation, affinity, faith, loyalty, friendship, and commitment.

A Romantic love goes through eight stages to become mature love

1. **Liking ('I' before 'you'):** The beginning of love begins with liking ('I' before 'you'). There is a boy and a girl who get to know each other better. It can be considered the beginning of a friendship. Even when they look at each other or are noticed by each other, they feel good. "I like you." The word 'I' is crucial here.

2. **Physical Attraction (I and You):** When liking is enhanced a little bit, it leads to physical attraction. During the process of loving oneself, he begins to love her as well. Physical attraction is caused by a strong urge to satisfy bodily demands. Physical attraction is a part of love, but it is not exclusive to it. Physical attraction can sometimes turn into love, but what is perceived as love can also be physical attraction. It is important for all of us to understand this. How does physical attraction work? There is an impulsive nature to it. There is impatience in it. Selfishness is involved. It is egotistical. There is a strong urge to satisfy bodily demands. When indulged in secretly, it can be thrilling. Daily routines may be disrupted as a result. In contrast, there is no serious thought, patience, perseverance, or a strong desire for a complete relationship. While 'you' and 'me' are important, 'I' is preferred over 'you'.

3. **Companionship to love (we two):** In the pre-marriage and early post-marriage periods, this love blossoms. The journey of 'we two' begins as closeness and develops a higher emotional level. Love transcends physical attraction and touches other deeper dimensions. Friendship and companionship gradually blossom into love.

    The example of a stork (saras) illustrates how love blossoms through companionship. Indian culture considers the stork a symbol of love. Some communities in Rajasthan and Gujarat send newlywed couples for stork-darshans. This could be an attempt to teach newlyweds how to develop their love through togetherness. We are now starting to move away from the 'I' before 'you' phase and towards a 'we two' phase.

4. **Romance *'Pranay'* (we two form a union):** Pranay means 'affinity' in Sanskrit. In addition to physical love, partners become emotionally involved as well. An emotional connection becomes as important as physical pleasure, and a strong connection develops naturally. As a result of this evolved togetherness, many things naturally arise. The feeling of 'oneness' is developed here. Romance is expressed through friendship, touch, silence, and physical satisfaction. *The Atharva Veda contains Pranaya Suktas. In Pranay mantras, the unity, togetherness and oneness of husband and wife are discussed and depicted.*

    Satisfaction, not greed, tender touch, not animal instinct, pleasant feeling of enjoyment, not forceful act, affinity, not ownership or authority, divine relationship, not demeaning attitude, possessiveness, not pride, steadfastness, not flirting, selfless, not selfish, bliss, not bragging, are the emotions at this

stage. It is at this point that both parties feel a strong bond and a sense of oneness.

5. **Commitment ('You are for me' and 'I am for you')**: It is a bond, but we must interpret it in a broader context. There is progress wherever there is a bond. Partner commitments are not compelled or forced, but voluntarily and wholeheartedly accepted by both parties. Devotion, loyalty, and trust are expected. Giving each other confidence that 'I am there for you' is what it is all about. In a commitment, contribution takes precedence over expectations. It is more important to give than to receive. Satisfaction comes from giving. The relationship becomes suffocating if the commitment is not up to par.

   Like a river, life is full of ups and downs. To flow between two banks, a river needs two banks. A sound relationship also requires a strong commitment between the partners. Living together in harmony requires effective channelization of this energy, and commitment is a prerequisite for effective channelization. A husband is committed to his wife, a wife is committed to her husband, and the family bond is strengthened by commitment. Commitment depends on our skills. The more the commitment to the project, the greater the partners' capacity, energy, and happiness. (We have already discussed the essential skills for the partners and how to acquire them.) Partners realize they need each other at this point.

6. **Surrender in love (first you and then I)**: In a relationship, surrender is letting go of the 'I' in oneself. As close as possible to reverence, the feeling should be sacred. When the partner supersedes 'self' in the relationship, this should come naturally

and effortlessly. Only when we love, respect, and care for our partner unconditionally can we achieve happiness. It is probably the power of surrender in love that makes this possible. This is why it is innocent and selfless. When you have a sense of dedication, difficult things become easier. The loss of 'I' in oneself is not an injustice to him, it is giving the relationship due justice. It is a two-way street, so dedication must come from both sides. Walking hand-in-hand along the path of dedication is very easy. In this journey of marriage, it is 'first you, then me'.

7. **Matured Love (we two make our world):** Time should be given to partners. Their love should flourish and mature so that it becomes mature love. The love between the partners is not incomplete, but rather leads them towards completeness. Forgiveness is part of love. Having an all-around, complete relationship is more important than just having a physical relationship. The mature love you experience develops you as an individual. 'You and I are different individuals' ends here, and a sense of oneness is developed. There is a sense of 'we cannot live without each other'.

    There are several factors that contribute to this type of love, including closeness, commitment, and trust. A love like this may be referred to as an ideal love. The type of love where the partners are in love with each other all the time is not very common. To attain and maintain this type of love, constant efforts are necessary. In the second milestone of love, we discussed this topic.

8. **The Ultimate Love (only you):** Sacrifice is at the core of this sublime love. As the consideration of 'the I in myself' ends,

only the thought of the partner remains. It is difficult to attain and even more difficult to maintain this kind of love. Here we are tempted to use the example of the stork. Once the stork chooses a partner, he spends most of his time with her. The stork also ends his life if she dies. As a result, 'the I in myself' is completely sacrificed, and only the consideration of the partner remains.

What can we learn from these stages?

The eight steps of love represent eight different shades of love experienced by couples at different points in their lives.

- The colour-shades are all enchanting; therefore, each stage should be enjoyed.
- Each colour-shade should be understood completely and viewed with an open mind.
- As one goes through each stage, one should enjoy it and remember that this stage is temporary, and the goal is to attain ultimate love. Many factors must be balanced for it to be successful.
- It is difficult to maintain the ultimate love. In order to accomplish this uphill task, both partners must work hard. Couples should make friends with the six supports of love: kindness, sensitivity, tolerance, joy, acceptance, and interest.

How to Express Love:

There is no universally accepted definition of a 'language of love'. Love can sometimes be difficult to express in words. Repeating 'I love you' is not enough to express love. Love cannot be measured by words. Words are a reflection of the apparent emotional mindset. Love originates in the heart. The vibrations

of the love language reflect the inner emotional mindset. Words cannot always express love as well as eyes.

The power of a glance is greater than the power of words. It helps one understand the language of the mind. The mind expresses itself through the eyes. The evidence of love is endorsed by a glance of love.

In many cases, actions express love, and what is not spoken is also understood. An expression of love like this creates a happy feeling and strengthens a relationship. Love can be expressed through words, eyes, and behaviour.

Individuals have their own mind set, their own way of thinking, and their own way of behaving. One's love and expression of love are also unique.

The five languages of love, according to Gary Chapman, are words, behaviours, gifts, spending time together, and touch. (Pl. ref. to 'Swayam 365' by Dr Pratibha Deshpande 4th month, 3rd week.)

Individual preferences may differ, but all love languages are normally used. While some may think a hug is important, others may think saying 'I love you' is more effective. As we grow older and circumstances change, our preferences may change as well.

Due to the nature of their work, Sushma and Bhalchandra were unable to stay together. Even at sixty, staying together is their definition of love.

There is nothing better than when the love languages of both partners coincide. However, if it differs, it may lead to a drift because the partner's expectations aren't met. When expectations are met, love blossoms, and if expectations aren't met, disappointment results. To cultivate love, partners must understand and accept

each other's love language. A change in the accepted love language may be brought about by circumstances. Such a change should be appreciated by partners. For example, Krishna may expect Radha to sit by his side when he is not feeling well.

It is not necessary to promise the moon to express love. Love can be expressed through things that will be liked, cherished, and remembered.

Love is expressed in various ways:

- Love is treating your partner with respect and trust.
- There are five types of intimacy in which love can be experienced. These are: sexual, emotional, mental, social, and intellectual.
- It is love when the beloved is assisted in his/her development and progress.
- Hugging a tired partner after a long day at work is love.
- Talking to one's wife and lending a hand when she's busy with household chores is love.
- Love is the ability to overlook one another's shortcomings.
- Sexual desire and other feelings are reflected in the eyes. Faith and trust are conveyed through the eyes.
- In order to express her love, a partner cooks a simple dish with love.
- Satisfaction in sexual relations acknowledges love.
- In love, one expresses gratitude for the partner's contributions to one's success.
- Writing letters of appreciation in one's own handwriting is a sign of love.
- E-mail and WhatsApp, the new technologies available today, can also be used to express love.

- Love is expressed by listening patiently to your spouse, taking a positive interest in him, offering positive inputs whenever necessary, and sparing exclusive time for him despite your busy schedule.
- Appreciating a partner's hard work is also a way to express love.
- Pats on the back, magical hugs, special tones of respect, smiles keep love alive.
- When supported by genuine feeling and trust, there are some magical expressions like 'Please' and 'I understand'.
- In love, the partner is shown confidence and trust, indicating that he is the most important person for her.

It's an endless list and it varies from person to person. There are some tips that seem insignificant and pointless, but never-the-less important. When the wife is in the kitchen, one may wonder if a kiss is appropriate. It's a way to show appreciation.

Case study: One day-old marriage

It was eleven o'clock in the morning,

An eighteen-year-old girl came with her father.

"This is my daughter and she wants a divorce," said her father.

"Sir, this is not a court. You will have to go to court for this."

"We went to court but they say separation can be done only after one year of marriage."

"That's right. How long has she been married?"

"Only for a day, ma'am."

"Yesterday!"

"Yesterday? And immediately she wants to get separated?"

"Her marriage was a cheated one."

The girl started crying. The father sat down in a chair in despair.

"I don't know what to do."

What went wrong, that she separated from the boy within a day?

"Sir, you will have to wait a year."

They were given water to drink. I expected them to go by now. But they were not ready to go. Even the father's eyes were watery.

"Shall I talk to you in detail?" asked the girl.

"Please speak."

This was her story. She was the only daughter of her parents. Both parents were employed. She was always alone and bored at home. Since she was in class 7, she used to go to school in a boy's rickshaw. The boy used to chat with her. And then they fell in love. For five years that boy sowed the seeds of love. She believed him one hundred percent. He showered her with gifts. The girl thanked him for removing her loneliness. He captivated her and wrapped around her, his web of love.

"Girl, why you did not tell your parents?"

"I was afraid that my family wouldn't have liked it."

"Why?

"Because he is uneducated, lower class but earns a lot of money. He cares for me."

"In what way?

"He asked me whether I was eating well, he took me to expensive hotels and showered me with gifts. He has always told me that I should complete my education, get a higher degree as he was deprived of education."

"Why?"

"Poverty. He was poor before and now he needs to support his family."

"Why did you feel he was concerned about you?"

"He recognized my mood instantly."

"Why you aren't in a good mood?"

"Sometimes it feels sad. Then he takes me to the cinema, gives me gifts."

"Physical intimacy?"

"..."

"Where?"

"At a hotel!"

"Since when?"

"It's been two years."

"What happened yesterday, when you got married?"

"Yesterday he cried a lot with me. He said, 'I am afraid. you will leave me I can't live without you, I will die.' I convinced him and said, 'Will you believe me if we get married?' He said, 'Yes.' He has a lot of trouble at home. Then I felt sorry for him. I love him so much, so...."

She stopped talking, tears in her eyes, her father was distressed.

"So, are you married?"

"Yes."

"Where?"

"In the temple of Alandi."

"Then?"

"I went to his house after marriage and his wife and two-year-old daughter were in the house."

"..." It was as if she were digging her own grave.

"What have you done!" screaming her father ran towards her as if he wanted to kill her.

"Did you know he was married?" I asked the girl.

She kept silent.

"So you knew. Why did you marry him?"

"He said he got divorced two years ago."

"Do you know what a big mess you've made?"

"..."

"Did he take wedding photos?"

"Yes!"

"Do you have copies?"

"No."

I was numb.

"There's nothing I can do about it."

From a perspective of a counselor:

This happened five years ago.

After that the girl kept coming for counselling.

She was in twelve std when she came, now she is an engineer. She divorced two years ago. She's a brilliant girl, did her GRE with a high score. Now she is going to America for further education. I appreciate her. She was doing whatever I said. She was facing society with confidence and talking about her mistake.

"One thing I learned from my mistake is that we are the cause of our downfall. Doctor, you taught me how to live, how to behave.

I remember what you said, 'Learning from what happened is an experience. You will get many such experiences. Wake up, we don't have time to cry. Every mistake has a correction. If correction is taken in the right way, it leads to improvement, otherwise it is destined to decline.'"

Today she has become a good friend of mine even if she is fifty years younger than me.

Case Study: With age, love grows and with time, it binds two souls.

The story is about an elderly couple, Malati and Vishnu.

Malati spent many years ill with arthritis. Years passed, and the time came when she was chained to the bed. The boys in America said, "Let's keep a maid." Vishnu understood Malati's expression and told the boys, "No maid. She did everything for me for so many years. Now it's my turn."

The maid was kept for cooking and other chores. Bathing her, taking her to the toilet, changing her clothes, feeding her, reading to her, everything was happily taken upon himself. For him, a walk in the morning for one hour was the routine and for the rest of the twenty-three hours, he was engaged with Malati.

Ten years, eleven months, three days passed. Then Vishnu got Alzheimer's.

Seeing the irony of the whole episode, when Malati passed away, he was not aware of the tragic incident as he did not recognise her as his beloved wife.

Looking at her dead body, he asked his son, "Who is she? Why she is lying?"

From the perspective of a counsellor:

- Was it nature's arrangement to take away his memory so that he wouldn't become sorrowful?
- The universe has its own answers, but for me, it was the love between him and her that connected them.
- There is something very precious about this pair.

The natural meaning of male-female intimacy is reproduction.
HE made a big plan to make it happy and happier.
Named it love and romance. Its meaning is simple,
humans should survive on earth,
but for us it is union of soul and body.

Section
6

Voices of Parents

1. Parental Role

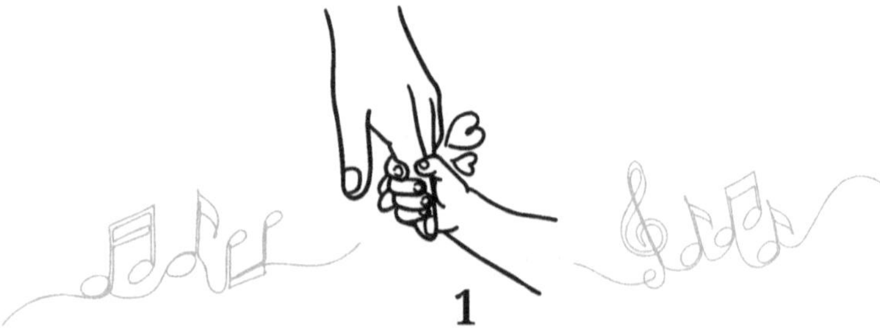

1

Parental Role

"Let parents bequeath to their children not riches, but the spirit of reverence!" Plato.

Parents play an important role in raising children. Most of all parents provide good education and facilities to their children. The love parents have for their children knows no bounds. They do everything in their power to raise their children well. But it can be said that the best parenting is practiced by the parents who teach their children good values and make them good human beings.

Things I feel as a counsellor:

From the cases coming for counselling, it is seen that disturbances in family system, increasing rate of break-up between lovers and live-in relationship, increasing rate of divorce in marriages, multiple partners, increasing cases of adultery, conflicts between spouses, expectations from parents, pressure from in-laws, infertility rates are increasing day by day. Suicide, stress, mental illness and mental problems are on the rise. Of course, the changing mentality of the society is the main reason for this. Apart from this,

there are still other reasons which are not in our hands to change. But why should we sit idly and look helplessly at the results?

We need to face the current situation, to come out of it safely and be happy.

What can you do? Can children still be raised wisely? To prevent further damage, it is important to identify these problems early and solve them. These times require wise parenting.

What is wise parenting?

Wise parents take care of all the physical, emotional, and mental needs of their children. Wise parenting involves loving, understanding, and guiding children as well as imparting good values and beliefs, creating a safe environment around them and teaching them patience, discipline, useful life skills. In short, parents should do everything for the children until they are able to take care of themselves, that is, until they are wise enough.

What should we do to make our children wiser?

Just as we give them good education for their intellectual growth, good healthy food for their physical health, we can teach them some valuable inputs for their mental growth.

- **Good human values:** Those who are good human beings will automatically learn and gain knowledge and wisdom. A good human being will make a good son/daughter, a good partner, or a good parent. In any relationship, he or she will be true to himself or herself. He/she will be kind and caring towards others. In addition to being a good citizen, he will contribute to the growth of the nation and serve as a role model for others.

- **Beauty:** Teach the true meaning of the word beautiful. Teach the beauty of behaviour and thoughts.

- **Emotional Intelligence**: Teach them to manage their own emotions. It is a skill that we need to use till our last breath. Research has also shown that EQ is more important than IQ to succeed in life.

- **Open-minded communication:** This is a skill that, once born, stays with you for life. Teach children to respect the person in front of them and communicate sincerely with no hint of arrogance. First, we need to understand when to speak clearly and when not to speak. "I have a strong opinion," may not always be a sign of wisdom. We have no right to insult another person with our words. Such personalities are intense.

- **Evolved personality:** The five-factor model of personality or OCEAN Traits is world famous. In this 'O' is openness i.e., acceptance of new experiences. Don't reject what you don't know. If you want a new experience, you should try what is new, for that you should open all the windows and doors of the mind and this mindset can be taught to children from childhood. 'C' stands for Conscientiousness which is the tendency to be self-disciplined, act conscientiously and strive to achieve against measures or external expectations. 'E' is Extraversion, how happy other people are in your company. 'A' denotes agreeable, how pleasant our personality is and how much we understand others and respect their opinions. 'N' is Neuroticism or emotional instability. It is a tendency to have strong negative emotions, such as anger, anxiety, or depression.

Children's personality depends on their parentage and home environment.

- **Importance of time:** If children are taught planning from an early age, they will develop an attitude towards valuing their time and that of others too.
- **Creativity:** Innovation, creativity, ingenuity should be inculcated from childhood.
- **Management of thoughts:** Truthfulness of thinking, avoidance of excessive thinking, emotional, rational, theoretical, logical, practical, creative, critical and deep thinking are inculcated in children from an early age.
- **Compromise, acceptance and adaptation**: First compromise and then accept good and bad experiences, situations, and people.
- **Ways of solving problems:** While living life, we are faced with numerous problems. One who has the skill to find their answer will find life easy.
- **Proper respect for both sexes:** We are taught in childhood to respect elders, we should go beyond that and respect every human being whether he/she is young or old. Men and women have unique qualities that should be respected.
- **Decision-making ability:** A person with this skill usually does not make mistakes or knows exactly what to learn from mistakes. Teach them to take responsibility for their decisions.
- **Willingness to do any work:** Be it a boy or a girl, children should be taught household chores. For example, cooking, cleaning, and taking care of siblings. If these things are taught from a young age, they know that there is no difference between siblings as boys/girls, but everyone has the responsibility of

household chores. Working together in a family also helps one to get used to helping each other and working together. This is important in the present new era as both are earning money together.

- **Gender difference:** Gender difference is one of the main causes of conflict in symbiosis. This creates a sense of dissonance in couples. A woman's self-esteem suffers because even after having a career like men, society still expects a lot from her. As a result, in many families, emotional and psychological problems can arise. It is very necessary to remove the social and cultural differences which are now showing their face with intensity. For this, children should be made aware from childhood. Children and especially boys should not be allowed to inculcate this discrimination in them from childhood. The environment in the home should be such that boys and girls understand that regardless of their gender, they must do whatever they have to.

When your children grow up, how do you want them to be?

The rules for parenting a young child and parenting when children are older, wiser, and mature are different. When children are older, it is time to see how the children are practicing what they have been taught them so far, now the days of their exams have come.

Let's trust the children, trust our parenting, and quietly watch them from afar. But in that case, we should avoid some mistakes. Some parents think that their children should not make the same mistakes that they did, or they know more than their children because they have seen a few more monsoons than them, but it

is very wrong because we have experiences according to our time or personality. Why we should limit them? Let them experience, make their mistakes, they will conquer the world. Don't limit their experiences. We know about ourselves, let them know more than us.

- We don't want to make children puppets in our hands by giving similar advice or preaching to them. And don't expect them to listen to you.
- The temptation to interfere with them should be avoided.
- Wise parents should communicate openly and honestly with their children as they mature and respect their opinions, understand their reasonable expectations, and give them an idea of their capabilities. Good parents participate in their children's lives and give them the right guidance and support when they need it. In doing so, it gives them their freedom and autonomy and makes them responsible.

Does parental involvement end when children get married?

When the child gets married, his new life begins. The role of a parent changes here. Here, there is a gap between two generations but if things are done properly it leads to a happy and harmonious life. This is the sweetness of life. Correct? Let's take a look at Suresh and Savitri as an example. The wisdom of parenting will be revealed through this pairing.

Case Study:

Suresh and Savitri have two children. He had brought up both his sons wisely so that when they grew up, they would become good men and good partners. They would take care of their partner, respect their opinions, and treat them as

equals. No wonder both the boys are successful in their business and in their relationship.

Savitri and Suresh did not interfere in the lives of the children after their marriage, did not do anything that would cause emotional or any stress. They believed, "Our children can live their lives properly. We have taught them that they should decide how to spend their lives. We will advise or help them whenever they need our help. We will support them, but only when they ask for it. Whatever progress they want to make, they should make their own decisions. It is important that they take responsibility and learn everything independently."

Savitri and Suresh started living separately from the children. They began to spend their lives happily as proud parents. Their children are also happy living independently with their spouses.

From a perspective of a counsellor:

- This is a classic example of wise parenting.
- Giving good education to children is a partial battle won but inculcating good values, sense of responsibility and religion is a complete battle won. Here, religion means their duties.
- Parents are always there to support their children, even when the children grow up. But parents should extend a helping hand only if necessary.
- If the life of the parents is happy and harmonious, it has a positive effect on the relationship of the children.
- Parents should reduce their authority over their children. Children are capable of new relationships, responsibilities and fulfilling expectations.

- There is a need for harmony in the family. Parents' expectations of their son and daughter-in-law should be openly and fully discussed. Parents should help the child list his expectations. Sometimes those expectations are not correct / not useful in practice. For example, if a child hands over his salary to his parents, parents should reject it. They should tell him, "Now you have grown up. This is the time for you to understand financial matters. You decide how much to spend, where to save."

Coexistence of children and parents
In Romantic Love:

Children sometimes realize that their child is having a love affair at an immature age or even in the early stages of consciousness. In such a case, one should communicate with children very carefully.

- Ask children directly. In that case, the parent with whom the children can communicate more should take the initiative. That is, if the child talks more openly with the mother, the mother should ask him directly.

- To this the children will probably give a dismissive answer. If there is no change in answer after asking twice, avoid asking them again. Avoid the temptation to talk to their friends at such times.

- If you keep a close eye on him without his knowledge, some things may come up. His behaviour, talking on the phone too much, going out for no reason, and many more such acts are indicators. If the child is feeling/acting differently from the way he/she used to behave for a while, it is not proof that it is a

love affair, because children who have come of age also behave differently.

- Parenting children of this age these days is very stressful. Yet if we raise children wisely, the challenges are less.

- If children openly talk about their love, listen quietly. Don't oppose it otherwise, the children will not speak further. They want to feel that their parents understand them.

- After they have spoken, say, "Look, you're acting your age, but this is unexpected, so I'll think about it, and then we'll get back to talking about it."

- If possible, children should elicit information about their chosen partner. If they feels it is right, then they should sit down and/or call the parents of the other partner and have a proper discussion. If children are convinced about the importance of education, they will complete their education and choose a career before settling down. When parents came to know about Sarika and Pawan's love, both told their parents that they were going to settle their careers and then get married. And they did it. In that case, the culture we impart to them, the teachings we give the children, the skills taught to them, all come in handy.

- The question arises when the wrong partner is chosen. In such cases the problem must be solved very delicately. But if there is wise parenting, children listen to readily. But if they are not open to discussion, then you have to plan differently. In such a case, one should be ready to seek the help of a counsellor.

- In some cases, children do not listen and then resort to running away etc. In such a case, parents should show their readiness to accept their relationship, else they will run from

their house to be with their partner. In this case, we may lose our child. If we approve of their partner and if something goes wrong with our child, at least we can help their child. I remember a case here. A girl from a good family ran away and married a very poor man. But her parents accepted them and kept them in their home and helped them complete their education. The girl's father also helped his brother financially by employing him. Of course, it was a lot of trouble, but today both of them lead a good life.

- Children are part of us, it is our responsibility to guide them when they are older and make mistakes.

Live-in relationship:

How should parents react when they find out that their child has chosen the path of a live-in relationship to be with his/her partner? This question is important. Everyone needs company at some point in life. The concept of a live-in relationship is not new. They have been around for decades; however, they are now becoming widely popular and openly discussed.

The mentality of the society is still not ready for this. Are live-in relationships more prevalent only among younger generations? The answer is no. Some people who are single (may be widows/widowers) and have settled children also enter live-in relationships in their older years just for companionship. They don't want to get married to avoid legal trouble with their own children.

Parents should not feel that they have done anything wrong in bringing up their child. Indeed, no parent wants their children to be in any relationship without any commitment. But once children become adults, these are their independent decisions and there

is no need to question their upbringing. Children are capable of making their own decisions and being independent. Parents should express their views, but they should not impose their ideology on children because their children will not understand at that time.

There is always a generation gap, and times change and so we have to accept what is best for us. A live-in relationship eventually brings two people together. It may or may not always be favourable. But when a live-in relationship goes wrong or goes sour, parents should stand by the children and pull them out of it.

- Talk openly with children. Listen carefully to what they say.
- If possible both sets of parents should meet, i.e., with their children's permission.
- Suggest the path of marriage to the couple. If the married life of the parents of both is good, then the children may be ready for marriage.
- If one partner's parents do not have a good marital life, he may not be willing to marry. Of course, at this stage, it's all ifs.
- If the children opt out, accept their decision happily with an open mind.

Love Marriages:

Many of these steps are similar to love affairs and live-in-relationships. Love marriages are generally opposed on the basis of looks, caste, education, as well as economic status and family environment. Parents' opposition is due to their concern for their child. Effective communication is essential here. Children should be given an opportunity to present their views before any decision is taken. Parents must tell their children about the possible dangers

of such a marriage. There should not be opposition on the issue of caste.

- Prioritize children's choices. At such times, put aside your opinion and let him be. Caste, age difference, education, difference between two cultures, nothing is more important than your child's happiness.

- Happiness in cohabitation does not depend on any of these. Spouses with a gap of twenty-five years, a great difference in education, and no financial equality can live a very happy life together.

- We should have only one goal in mind and that is the happiness of children. No mother or father can decide what makes a grown child happy. Here is a case as an example: Shantabai is constantly upset with her daughter-in-law. Her son had married for love and now he sits and cries. After looking at all the aspects, the boy said, "The reason why I am crying is not my wife but my mother who annoys my wife a lot and drives me emotionally crazy. I am constantly being teased for being a cat under my wife's plate. My wife is very thoughtful and just what I want. But my mother does not allow us to live happily." And if the child chooses the wrong partner, let him take responsibility for it, but don't scold him.

- Parental Involvement in Children's Love Marriage: Love marriages are generally opposed on the basis of their looks, caste, education, as well as economic status and family environment. Parents' opposition is due to their concern for their child's happiness. Effective communication is essential here. Children should be given an opportunity to present their views before any decision is taken. Parents must tell their

children about the possible dangers of such a marriage. There should not be opposition on caste.

- Parents should understand that a man in love cannot think rationally. So, if the children are not ready to change their decision, accept it. Parents should, however, explain the dangers involved.
- Parents should listen carefully to children.
- If parents think something is wrong, then they should explain its dangers.
- But after marriage, if it doesn't work out for some reasons, parents should support their children unconditionally without holding them guilty. Parents should not point out the child's mistakes later.
- Here the role of good parenting starts. When the time comes to find a partner, they will find a partner who is right for them. Psychiatrists say that inadvertently a boy looks for his mother in a partner and a girl looks for her father in a partner. Therefore, parents influence the decisions of children unknowingly.
- Let us love our children unconditionally. Forgive their mistakes. This will help them to get out of this situation.
- Parents should provide facilities for their children that will be useful in times of trouble. For example, a fixed deposit should be made in the name of the daughter, because if the daughter goes abroad after marriage and there are some difficulties, then the funds for return will be facilitated.

Arranged Marriage:

We have already talked a lot about this in the 2nd section.

- Talk to children and ask for their expectations. If their expectations are not right, give your opinion.

- Finally let the children decide. Parents can give them some suggestions, if necessary, but they cannot tell them or force them.

- Parents have strong expectations from their daughter or son-in-law. Those expectations will not be fair if they are compared to the daughter or son-in-law of their relatives or friends.

- As times change, parents should also change. If the son/daughter refuses a match, there is stress in the family. If there is open discussion, the boy/girl will be able to tell his/her reason for rejection. If the reason doesn't make any sense (e.g. daughter is a lawyer and has a habit of arguing due to her profession), parents should try to persuade, not insist.

- Although old people say that 'marriages are made in heaven', the boy/girl who wants to spend life together should be given a chance to get to know each other. It is more important whether they feel right for each other than whether the horoscope matches or not.

- Harmony and understanding between both the families are very important in an arranged marriage. The wedding is an important milestone in everyone's life, and everyone wants to celebrate it well, but at what cost?

- Rather than prioritizing material things, it is important to see if you have another family with similar thoughts. So, harmony is the key to everything.

- There should be proper communication between both the families regarding the expectations of the girl/son. Divorce within six months is very high among couples who get married

this way. This is due to ideological differences between the two, pre-marital affairs, suspicion, misinformation, fraud. So, the parents must give proper time between *Sakharpuda* (engagement) and marriage to develop understanding.

- As mentioned in the previous chapter, this time will be used to resolve the above-mentioned matters. They may refuse to marry if they know some concealed information. Isn't this better than divorce after marriage?

Involvement of parents after the marriage of their child:

Something is bound to change when two youngsters decide to spend their lives together. Both the parents should accept that change. Both sides have different feelings regarding this event. A romantic relationship is not a blood relationship. And the main thing is that before the relationship is formed, the personality of both the partners is formed including their moral values. There is a school of thought that the relationship between daughter-in-law and mother-in-law should be like that of a mother and daughter, but it must be kept in mind that this is not possible. Both these relationships are different and should be accepted as they are. A daughter-in-law will be a daughter-in-law, and a mother-in-law will be a mother-in-law, but this does not necessarily imply that she will not perform well as a daughter. Even though she can be as good as a daughter, why should they label her as a daughter, why can't they say that their daughter-in-law is good? It's the same way with the mother-in-law. They can be great friends, it's true.

- A girl is expected to accept the boy's culture, life style and traditions. What's wrong with her accepting the tradition of her husband's family? No, it should be accepted. Symbiosis is

a union of mind and body. Then there should be a union of culture and tradition.

- It is not right to expect a girl to work in an office and then do all the household chores. A boy should also contribute to the household chores and create harmony in their life. Thus, if both take the responsibilities equally, they will be able to live a happy and harmonious life by avoiding the difficulties that may arise.

- In olden days it was said that once a girl was married, she belonged to the family till death. Does that mean she has no right to where she was born and where she grew up?

- A girl is equally responsible for her parents. But this doesn't this mean that her family should interfere in the girl's life and take decisions for her. The girl's parents should act responsibly and advise the girl only when she needs it. They should give moral support to the girl but also recognize their limits.

Role of parents in separation of children:

Sometimes a situation arises where things are out of hand, and both have decided to separate.

Separation is a very delicate matter and the whole house gets traumatized. The decision is very difficult but sometimes we must accept it.

Although the decision belongs to both the spouses, it affects the parents of the spouses too.

- No parent can bear to see their children sad or disappointed. There are many reasons for separation, but it is important that they boost their children and support them.

- Because children think differently, it is important to give them emotional support and advice in these situations.
- Spending time with them, going on trips, chatting, asking for help from a counsellor, having a pet, going to the cinema, talking about their childhood interests, encouraging them to learn more, asking them to participate in public activities, etc. can help them overcome their grief.
- During this period many people / relatives will talk about their separation and blame them. But parents should stand by their decision and give moral support at such times. They should stick to their decisions and not take unwanted advice.
- Parents should support their children in their grief but not allow them to drown in grief.

Parents' role in infidelity:

Acts of infidelity not only traumatize the other partner but also the parents and family of both sides. The life of both the families can be ruined.

- Initially parents are not aware of their children's unfaithful acts.
- Parents of a person involved in infidelity may feel guilty and question their parenting.
- Dissatisfaction arises in the family.
- What should be the role of parents if either partner is unfaithful? Obviously, when children grow up, they are independent and take all the decisions and the role of parents in such activities is negligible.
- If parents come to know about their children's infidelity, they must discuss it openly with them without hesitation. If the

child is not in a position of open expression with his parents, he should seek help from close family members/friends or counsellors. The act of cheating on the other partner is very painful. In such cases, parents should help them, stand firmly by their side.

- If necessary, they should be strict with their own children as infidelity should not be encouraged as it will affect future generations as well.

- Parents may have two different reactions: they may initially be angry with their children but knowingly/unknowingly they may support their children's acts of infidelity or they may cut ties with their children.

- Whatever decision children take, support them but don't interfere or give advice or take decisions on behalf of children.

Children:

Your partner's parents are blood relatives of our beloved one. They have taken care of him much before he came into your life. They should be properly respected. If you don't get along with them, no problem, but you have no right to object to your partner taking care of them.

Do not mix up the roles, parents are parents and partners are partners. A mother is a mother, and a wife is a wife. The position of both is different. Don't expect your female partner to do what your mother is doing for you.

Keep in mind that behind every relationship there is a person. Cherish that person. Preserve that person instead of trying to mend the relationship. Automatically, the relationship will be preserved.

Parents:

You can trust your parenting. You don't need to give them advice unless they ask for it. Allow them to make their own decisions and learn from their mistakes. Be available to them if they need advice and respect their decisions. Trust their judgement. Accept your children's partners as they are. Include them in your family. Give them as much love as an important family member. Respect them, love them.

Let's look at ordinary to extraordinary in the next chapter.

Parents who are proud of their children recognize their accomplishments,
no matter how small or insignificant they may seem.
Offer support when times are tough.
Show your children that you believe in them and that you
are proud of them,

Section 7

A Rhythmic Relationship

1. A Musical and Melodious Journey

1

A Musical and Melodious Journey

10 commandments for your melodious and harmonious relationships:

1. **Observe Innocence:** Innocence is the experience of not knowing, enjoying a fresh perspective of our partner. (Ref. 'Swayam 365' by Dr Pratibha Deshpande). Finding innocence in togetherness requires trust, vulnerability, and open communication. You can restore innocence to your relationship by regularly showing your partner how much you love and appreciate him or her. Hugs, kisses, and compliments can help create a sense of innocence and intimacy. Be open with your partner about your vulnerability by telling them about your fears, hopes, and dreams. Being honest with your partner is an excellent gesture. Communicate your feelings, concerns, and needs in a non-judgmental manner so that you can create a safe environment around your partner. By spending time together and engaging in activities you both enjoy like such as taking walks, going on dates, or just spending time cuddling and talking, you will be able to connect with your partner and bring back a sense of innocence and joy to

your relationship. The most important factor is to let go of past hurts, resentments and practice forgiveness. Grudges can create a barrier in your relationship and prevent you from experiencing true innocence and intimacy.

2. **Create your own world:** Being in a relationship doesn't mean that you must be with him/her all the time. Keep your own passions and interests alive by maintaining your individuality and independence. Create your own world according to your personal choices. To keep the relationship fresh and exciting, you need to be able to spend time apart. Enjoy your own world. Though it is important to stay connected and to communicate openly with each other, it is also important to be able to spend time apart to pursue your own interests. Keep in mind that your relationship should be based on two independent individuals, not a merging of identities. If you wish, you can share this world with your partner. You can discuss each other's worlds.

3. **It is okay to be beautifully selfish:** "Beautifully selfish" means prioritizing your own needs and happiness in a healthy and balanced manner. To help you accomplish this, here are some tips: Establish boundaries, take care of yourself, prioritize your goals, surround yourself with positive influences, practice self-compassion, prioritize your health, embrace your passions, focus on personal growth, align your actions with your values, and be true to yourself. Beautiful selfishness does not mean disregarding others' needs and feelings. You need to find a balance between taking care of yourself and being considerate of others.

4. **Eliminate stress:** Keep all your stress out of your home. For example, stress at workplace. This dangerous demon will ruin **your relationship.** When a couple is stressed, they may feel angry, frustrated, and resentful, which can lead to tension in their relationship. It can lead to a breakdown in communication, which can further escalate tensions. It is a dangerous demon in your life. (Ref. 'Before You Find a Counsellor' by Dr Pratibha Deshpande.)

5. **Keep aside stormy thoughts:** There is danger in stormy thoughts since they can cause negative feelings and thoughts. Our thoughts and emotions can lead us to act in ways that are not in our best interest, such as lashing out at others, engaging in destructive behaviors, or making decisions that could have serious consequences.

6. **Work on your 'Swayam' throughout your life:** The process of developing oneself is an ongoing one. Personal growth requires determination, focus, and commitment. You should act and strive to achieve your goals. Progress can be monitored through regular reflection and evaluation.

7. **Don't feel helpless:** Helplessness is acquired over time. A person learns it through repeated negative experiences, such as feeling overwhelmed by tasks or powerless in difficult circumstances. With helplessness, even small tasks can overwhelm a person, and they may have difficulty making decisions or acting. If you have learned helplessness, you should unlearn it. You are not a puppet in your partner's hands. Instead, stand shoulder-to-shoulder with him/her.

8. **Renew your relationship every day so that it won't become stale:** Together, try out new activities. Spending time together

in silence can be a wonderful experience. Just sit while holding each other's hand and say nothing. Just experience the warm touch of your partner.

9. **Avoid submissive behaviour:** Being submissive all the time is not a good choice. It will damage the relationship and can lead to feelings of resentment and anger. Requesting permission and giving feedback will ensure that both partners are aware of each other's needs and feelings.

10. **Don't go in a comfort zone:** Stagnation and lack of personal growth can result from staying in your comfort zone. Being in a comfort zone can bring staleness in you. Taking risks, trying new things, and stepping outside your routine can be inhibited by it. You may not have the opportunity to learn, develop, and reach your full potential as a result. Furthermore, staying in your comfort zone hinders your ability to adapt to new situations and challenges, making it harder to deal with adversity or navigate changes. It will definitely affect your relationship.

Counselor's note concludes the book:
Don't set unrealistic expectations for your partner
which you, yourself, can't meet. Be realistic and honest
about what you can and cannot do. In case it needs to be
adjusted, it is okay.

Make sure you do not wear your shoes all the time.
It's wonderful to put yourself in your partner's shoes.
Their viewpoints and feelings can be better understood.
Set no boundaries for them,
Let them breathe freely, don't dominate them.
Together, you'll be able to capture the sky.

Now, it's time to say Goodbye.

An Introduction to the Author, Dr. Pratibha Deshpande

Dr. Pratibha Deshpande is a counsellor, life couch and author. She has unparalleled experience in the field of counselling. In dealing with her seekers, she has developed her own innovative methods which help her to create rapport with them. Sessions with her are positive and comfortable. She creates a friendly environment in which seekers feel comfortable, sharing their thoughts and emotions. Her approach fosters trust between herself and the seekers, allowing them to engage more openly and authentically, resulting in a more effective and therapeutic relationship.

She is a living example for everyone. She serves as a role model for her peers and younger generations, inspiring them to never give up and strive for greatness. When asked about her age, she says humorously, "My age is just a convenience for me to live on my own terms."

According to her, 'life' is just a word. It is more important what you do with this word. Her definition of life is that it is a place where one can grow and evolve as an individual. She says that it›s okay to be beautifully selfish. Taking care of oneself is essential for taking care of others, so we should focus first on our own growth. She hopes that her work will inspire others to find their own path

to growth and fulfilment. A doctorate in psychological first aid and a master›s degree in psychology are among her qualifications.

Dr. Pratibha has written 18 books about human relationships and emotions. Her writing reflects a lot of her life and experiences. She has been invited to many radio programs to discuss psychology and relationships, where she shares inspiring stories and practical tips for personal growth.

Her recent book on self-growth, 'Swayam 365', won the publishers' first prize for useful and novel books.

She would love her readers to get in touch with her and give their feedback.